The Value of Corruption
in a Democratic Society

The Value of Corruption in a Democratic Society

How to Get Your Garbage Picked Up

A. Professor

Writers Club Press

San Jose New York Lincoln Shanghai

The Value of Corruption in a Democratic Society
How to Get Your Garbage Picked Up

Writers Club Press
an imprint of iUniverse.com, Inc.

For information address:
iUniverse.com, Inc.
620 North 48th Street, Suite 201
Lincoln, NE 68504-3467
www.iuniverse.com

ISBN: 0-595-12724-X

Printed in the United States of America

Preface

This book will expound a very simple thesis: that corruption is necessary for the efficient functioning of a free society. The reader must learn from these concepts if he is to have any hope of leaving something tangible to his grandchildren when he departs for other pastures, (maybe not greener).

I have studied and taught at universities for thirty five years, published over 120 articles in peer reviewed journals and edited three major textbooks. I have read hundreds of books, consulted thousands of news articles and spoken to a few inebriated politicians. Unfortunately none of these endeavors have anything to do with the current subject matter. However this stuff is really good.

We will study the methods of operation and orderly progression of day to day activities which are made infinitely smoother by a bit of grease. Of course this book may have a limited educational appeal, since the vast majority of free people know the score already. But for those souls who need some pointers in how to survive, the following chapters will be of service.

The mere act of getting from one day to the next may be an overburdening chore for many people, particularly if they make the mistake of opening their mail in the morning. By the time one discovers the extent of debts, or the response forms that should be filled out, or the number of one's friends in trouble, he can barely find the strength for the next coffee break. It is therefore vital never to compound the error by responding to anything that you have received in the mail. If it's really important, you'll be contacted in a more direct manner soon enough.

I usually keep three separate desk files organized according to priorities. The priorities are, of course inversely related to the time it takes for the contents to reach the waste basket. Therefore, at the outset, I will give all my readers one of my prime rules for making it in this society: Never answer any mail that is not a second notice (lower priority items can even await a third). This will lead to a fantastic saving of time, an invaluable commodity.

Do not be confused by the proliferating complexities of daily existence. They are merely devices that gave birth to a new burgeoning industry—the manufacture of garbage liners. As you will learn, life in a free society is really simple if you don't take things too seriously. Of course there may be a few poor people who are concerned about their next meal. To them I say, be of good heart, you will soon learn that you are an integral part of the republic. Assume your role with honor and pride, and above all adopt a strong belief in reincarnation.

Now just a word of warning to the unwary reader. You must have a salt shaker available as you absorb this text so as to guarantee a sufficient number of grains to enable you to complete it and still retain your sanity and composure.

Chapter 1

The Need For Corruption

Why should a democratic society be corrupt? This is, of course, a philosophical question and needs to be answered at a back table in a bar, over a pitcher of beer and some pretzels. The more logical question is: why is a democratic society corrupt?

The need for corruption stems directly from the fabric of the democratic society, which creates a constant flow of new laws. By its very nature the election of a congress or parliament will lead to a profusion of laws and ordinances. After all, it isn't likely that a senator could stand for reelection on the platform that things are so great in the country that no new laws are needed. No. Any illusion by the electorate that congress sat around all day discussing the baseball scores could lead to a rather distasteful appraisal of whether legislators were really needed at all.

Therefore, because we elect representatives, they have to prove they're doing something to earn their paychecks, so, they pass a bunch of laws.

One might add at this point that most of these representatives are lawyers to begin with[1], leading to an unpleasant feeling that the passage of all these laws may represent a conflict of interest. After all, they are uninterpretable by any standards except to the remaining partners in the congressman's law firm.

Laws serve a number of purposes, in addition to giving the appearance that congress is working and providing employment for a large segment of the legal profession. By their very nature they are restrictive. Things usually work out all right until laws are passed (after all, we arrived here through thousands of years of human existence without laws). Then we have a whole host of regulations about usage, restrictions, directions, new definitions, etc., which in the long run tend to screw things up. Corruption, therefore, serves as a means of circumventing these laws and getting things back on the right track.

An embarrassing question comes up: If the representatives really wanted to do a good job, why don't they pass laws that don't do anything?

Answer: The motives of the corruptor are pure and noble—to facilitate a better life for everyone in this society. But for the curruptee, although his is an integral role in the procedure, he pockets a bit of cash with the deal. This is not all bad since it guarantees that only fine minds and talented people will apply for those jobs that offer the best chances to be corrupted, and it relieves the tax burden.

---

[1] Seventy two and two thirds of our current congress are lawyers. The fractions represent a number who failed to pass the bar exam. J. Congressional Stats. 1998,Vol.2: pp219-220

But one wonders if some laws aren't passed in order to provide an opportunity for corruption to occur.

Judging the system as a whole, however, one must admit that it works well. If it didn't all the lawyers would have to become doctors, and God knows we've got too many of them already.

Therefore in summary:

A. The people have to be represented in government or they get very upset.

B. The representatives have to do something for a living so they pass laws.

C. Corruption is necessary to bypass the laws so the society can function properly.

The Way Things Work
(A lesson in a short conversation)

Sam Cohen hated furtiveness. As he quietly climbed the dark staircase he thought of his intense efforts all his life to be honest, open, frank and explicit with all of his business acquaintances, wife and children. He remembered his wife's stinging glances as she drank her gin and tonic, when he told his sixteen-year-old daughter that sex was not all that bad. (This elicited an immediate demand for an extension of her curfew to 2:00 A.M.)" If she gets knocked up I suppose I'll get blamed for that too" he thought. His wife tried to counter the argument by indicating that sex was not all that good either, which made Sam flinch. However, the gleam in his daughter's eye reasserted his role as the authoritative figure in the household.

But Sam had been that way since his childhood. He was a two sewer man at stickball and as such was charged with the responsibility of choosing up sides. He was always fair and sure to take the worst player on his side. This was usually Artie a future doctor and Stuyvesant graduate who had trouble seeing the ball, in spite of his thick glasses. Artie became a surgeon.

A small, sixty- watt bulb lit his way to the top of the stairs. "What shit," he thought, "I'm finally reaching a stage in life when I can relax and this crap has to happen". He felt the stab of pain around his hemorrhoids. "Oh," he groaned, "what shit."

Sam was in the importing business. Whenever some manufacturer was in trouble Sam was there to buy him out and place the goods where they could be easily turned over. Business was booming and expansion was in the works.

The narrow hallway led to several doors constructed of pitted wood as if they were meant to be a set in an old Sam Spade movie. Above one he noticed the name clearly imprinted on the glass: C.K. Chang, Lawyer.

What an understatement. Chang was the right-hand man of the mayor—decision maker, advisor, contact man. What the hell was he doing in a place like this?

Sam entered the small office. A short blonde girl with a 36D cup was seated at an oak veneer, decrepit desk. A 4 by 3 foot Picasso print hung on the wall immediately behind her with several scattered Utrillo prints of April showers on a Parisian street.

"You are expected, Mr. Cohen," she said. Her desk was bare except for a phone and a yellow scratch pad.

"No typing required" thought Sam. His wife was wrong as usual.

C.K. sat at an enlarged version of his secretary's desk in a room that was painted totally brown, with bare walls. Next to the desk was a wooden folding chair which was obviously meant for visitors. "A facade" thought Sam who had seen Chang in his city hall office surrounded by drapes, oriental statues, and flat-chested secretaries. Clearly, this office was meant to intimidate, to create an atmosphere of power. A respected businessman stooping to visit this atrocity of a business office would be acutely aware of his own impotence in the face of government.

Sam approached the chair facing Chang and noticed immediately the small round cushion with the hole in the center. " He even knows about my hemorrhoids, what efficiency."

"Mr Cohen, what can I do for you?"

"Bastard" thought Cohen as he felt the stab of pain in his anus. Twelve months without a sitzbath and now this. "Mr. Chang as you know, I'm a recent visitor to this part of the world and have operated a small business here for three years. Success has followed our opening and we have been trying to expand into a neighboring building. A number of strange occurrences have prompted my visit to see if we can facilitate our expansion. That is, whether you can help."

"Ah yessss," hissed Chang, "I am aware of your attempted expansion, and as you know the government is delighted to see the investment and expansion of capital into the deprived areas of our city."

"A pain in the ass," thought Sam, "the entire thing is a pain in the ass".

"I appreciate the efficiency of your city government," said Sam, "but I have run into certain problems which I've been advised to see you about."

"Perhaps if you reviewed these with me it might be possible to—ah— see if anything can be done."

"Well as you know we are expanding our business into a neighboring building. This, of course, requires the installation of new electrical wiring, plumbing, and so forth. In addition I was told that our help will demand a local toilet, although for the life of me I can't see why they can't walk next door."

"Well, who can account for the tastes of individuals," replied Chang. "Since private toilets appeared in our community, there is no satisfying the demands of labor."

"Of course," continued Sam, "there's carpentry work, reconstruction of rooms, moving of furniture, which must be finished by a specific time if we're going to expand and still make money."

"Ah yes, I understand," said Chang, "but certainly this can all be worked out. You must have allocated these responsibilities to expert help."

"Absolutely," replied Sam. "We hired Donovan and Sons to do all the work and they've supervised the designs, made all the arrangement, gotten the materials and permits and so forth. But there have been a series of unusual occurrences."

"Perhaps you can be more specific?"

"Well, twelve weeks ago I asked a sanitation department for special pickup of twelve cartons of trash lined up behind our present building. Last week as our plumbers unloaded their material the sanitation truck appeared and hauled away three toilets, two water coolers, and a bidet requested by the secretary of one of our senior partners. The trash is still there."

"How unfortunate," mused Chang, "I am sure that can be rectified."

"In addition, our electrical supplier arrived Wednesday to coordinate the wiring of our new addition and within ten minutes his truck with all his tools was towed away for illegal parking."

"But surely you must recognize the necessity for keeping traffic moving on the city streets."

"I know, I know, but he was parked in our parking lot—which, by the way, has received a notice of condemnation for having an entrance onto the city streets without a permit."

"Oh dear," said Chang, "city ordinance 12A-32 again—we must do something about that."

"It is apparent," said Cohen, squirming slightly in his cushioned chair, "that the only parking lots which are permissible are those that have no entrances or exits."

"I admit that this may seem like a strange regulation", said Chang, "but the parking lot industry is very powerful in this city."

"Then came the sewer department," Sam was really getting warmed up now, "For some ungodly reason it appeared that our furniture delivery service truck was parked over a proposed sewer site."

"Surely," said Chang, "a small problem. Easily solved by moving the truck a few feet either way."

"Not so simple "indicated Cohen, shifting his weight directly onto his right buttock. (In past years this had been responsible for the development of left hip pain, which in conjunction with his hemorrhoids led to an unusual position during movement of his bowels. His wife saw this once when she entered the bathroom looking for a hair dryer and entertained some unexplainable suspicion whenever Sam complained of anal pain thereafter.)

Sam continued, "It's the way we were notified that made things difficult. We were moving a desk to the second floor of the new building when we heard a resounding crash. People were rushing into the streets from all directions but there was no truck when we came downstairs. Only a large hole in the ground. It cost me four hundred dollars to hire a crane to retrieve the truck, and now I'm being sued for two late deliveries and obstructing a sewer."

"Ah yes, you do seem to have a few problems," replied Chang,. "It would seem that you are in need of a contractor."

"But we have Donovan and Sons. Aren't they licensed by the city? Surely they've built many projects in town. They're large and well respected." Sam was firing at fever pitch by now.

"All of that, all of that, Mr. Cohen. And in addition they are of the proper political persuasion."

As Chang talked Cohen became aware of the orientation of the Asian…The room was lit by a single central chandelier with two bulbs missing from its six sockets. "Adds to the degradation," Cohen thought. The brown walls reflected little of the light so that Chang sat facing him in semi darkness. But he was alive in his discourse on politics. Rimless glasses accented and enlarged his slanting eyes, wrinkling against the reflected light as he moved his hand from side to side.

"You see, those of us who have attained political power have struggled throughout the ranks of the discontented, the job seekers, the vote getters, the hangers-on. We paid our dues in obedience and hard work to attain an element of power. It is our job to make things run, and we mean to see that they don't run without us. Otherwise the system breaks down. Who would take a job as an assistant commissioner of buildings but an ineffi-cient malcontent? We have developed a more perfect system to guarantee efficiency by making the rewards satisfy the requirements of the job."

"Couldn't you just ask for a raise?" said Cohen. He was sorry immediately.

"Cohen, you must surely understand that nobody gives a damn what an assistant commissioner makes. The average person might grumble about paying a few cents more for a loaf of bread,—he just passes on the costs to his customers if he's in business, or through his union to his boss, who then passes it on to his customers. Everyone pays a little more and makes a little more and the system looks great. But a raise in salary to a city official would have to be passed on as an increase in taxes! You can tell your customers that your costs are high,—that they understand. But try to increase your prices because your income taxes are too high and see what they say about that."

How could you argue with such logic? thought Cohen. He was already figuring how the new building would increase his prices—Actually with a few cents extra he could make a neat profit. So it will cost a few dollars more...

"The political system and the economic system are intertwined. They each work for the mutual efficiency and satisfaction of all."

The little Chinese man had all the answers. Cohen could feel his bulbous hemorrhoid receding. He felt better already. In fact he was somewhat relieved to have the course of events safely in the hands of one who under-stood the system so well.

"Cohen, you need a contractor!"

"But I already have a contractor. What am I going to do with Donovan and his Goddamn sons?"

"You still don't understand. Donovan does his job, and he does it well. After all he has a lot of experience. He builds the building, gets the plumbers, the electricians, but you need a contractor for the others."

"The others?

"Of course. The sanitation department, the sewer department, the traf-fic department. I am offering the services of a political contractor who will handle the whole job."

"For how much?"

"Ten percent of the entire cost is the usual fee. I believe the addition is going to run in the neighborhood of four hundred thousand dollars. That will be forty thousand dollars.

With a bit of fast addition Cohen could see that this wasn't too bad. After all Donovan had wanted four twenty for the job and after hard bargaining he had gotten the lower price. Suppose he had been a schlemiel and paid the four twenty—so its close to the same thing.

"Of course we have a special package that includes the inspectors."

"The inspectors?"

"Well you have to be inspected by the Building Department, the Health Department, the Fire Department…"

"Oh my God." The rectal pain started over again and Cohen"s hip began to act up. "How much?"

"Well it's not too bad…It will cost an additional five percent, but this is a special package that will pay for itself."

"Pay for itself?" Cohen began to feel foolish for repeating the successive statements of Chang, but he couldn't seem to help himself.

"You see, in this package we include the city assessor. The new assess-ment rate will increase your property taxes by seven thousand dollars a year. We will arrange to lower your assessment to an additional three thousand a year. In five years the added package is paid off. After that we'll see."

If efficiency was a criterion of good government Cohen would have cast his vote with Chang at that moment. Amazing, he thought. This guy has everything figured out. The rewards of the office of assistant commis-sioner became painfully evident. Cohen thought of all the building going on in the city—what a deal—no wonder this guy worked so hard to get to this position. Cohen reached for his checkbook: "I suppose the blonde outside is the cashier?"

"Oh no, no. You will be notified as to where and how to provide payment."

Cohen sat back for a moment and sighed deeply. He'd moved from Brooklyn to this—He glanced slowly at Chang, amazed at the way the system was organized. The Chinaman at the center of the operation seemed appropriate to all he had heard and read about Asian societies. The dollar opened doors everywhere, but "why the hell did I have to move to Cincinnati?"

Chang extended his hand. The meeting was over.

Cohen rose and with the usual formalities started to back toward the door. His hemorrhoid fully receded, he was prepared to face the prospects of expanded business. What a system, he thought.

He was part way through the door when he turned slowly and faced Chang. "About the twelve cartons of trash..."

"Oh that," said Chang, "Just slip the sanitation driver twenty bucks."

Chapter II

Definitions[2]

1. **CORRUPT**: From the Latin cor=heart and rupt=break. Literally to break one's heart.

Sense: To strive through hard work, to accomplish great ends through diligence.

Common usage: Usually attributed to a more dependent portion of the male anatomy as: to break one's b———.

---

2. The Dictionary of Strange Derivations, Webster S.E. Britannia Publications, Belfast, Ire. 1848 3rd ed.

2 **CORRUPTOR**: One who corrupts. Necessitating great scheming to attain noble ends.

The corruptor is by definition always of a higher social standing than the corruptee.

Otherwise we have:

3. **BRIBERY**: The act of bribing. From the olde English briberry a form of poisonous berry grown around castles.

Sense: To give a gift to attain personal advancement. This is tried by one of low social standing to a higher authority. Usually greeted with disdain. In olde England usually met by forcing a briberry down the bloke's throat at the castle door.

4. **DEMOCRACY**: From the Latin demo=to show and cracere=cracks.

This usually refers to a form of government which everybody is convinced will crack up at any minute,…and is usually trying to change.

Sense: A form of government which allows its constituents to continually ask for change.

Common usage: A place where having money is not bad, and everyone thinks they may have some—someday.

5. **SOCIAL CLASS**: The social strata which determines where to shop for one's clothes.

This can be defined by a formula which gives the ratio of service/tips consistently at any good restaurant. The higher the ratio the higher the social class to which one belongs. It is evident by the definition that one cannot buy his way into an upper or higher social class. On the contrary the determination is made for him by any competent head waiter.

6. **SOCIETY**: Everybody else.

7. *INCORRUPTIBLE PERSON*: A good government advocate who failed political science in college.

8. *POWER*: The ability to corrupt.

In a free society the term "more power to you" is the highest form of good wishes one can muster—a quantum leap over "have a nice day".

9. *TAXES*: From the Hebrew "taches" referring to a certain anatomic region exposed as one reaches under his robe to get at his money belt.

A form of tribute which over the years has come to define social class structure. The worse the financial burden, the lower the social class. Ultimately the highest classes merely display their "taches" at the tax collectors, having no financial burden at all.

10. *TAX SHELTER*: Also from the Hebrew. Referring to a robe with hidden pockets which protected one's "taches" from the tax collectors.

Sense: To cover one's _ss.

Common Usage: Making the government your business partner.

11. *LEGISLATURE*: Derivation from the Latin: legitamus=the true or right; slatore=slate or roster.

Sense: The roster of the right. Referring to people of the right breeding, i.e. not needing employment for financial needs.

12. *PARLIAMENT*: From the Latin: parliere=to speak a=without; mentatus=to think.

Sense: A place where speaking without thinking is commonplace.

Common usage: Exactly!

13. *GOVERNMENT*: From the Neanderthal grave men. Certain individuals too incompetent for daily tasks were given the job of burying those members of the tribe bitten by a saber tooth tiger.

They subsequently demanded official burying places, better thoroughfares for dragging off dead bodies, and uniforms—thus being the first government.

Sense: An organization of garbage collectors.

Common usage: with law degrees.

Chapter III

Corruption V.S. Bribery

This chapter deals with a fundamental concept : the difference between corruption and bribery. Corruption implies an intensive effort to manipulate government for the general good. There is a clear understanding that a large profit will be involved with the subsequent development of jobs, new business efforts, further investments and improvement of society's well being.

Those instigating the corrupt act must by definition be of a higher social order than those being corrupted. Since in a republic the highest order of activity is making money, it therefore follows that businessmen will usually be at the core of most corrupt activities. This is as it should be, facilitating the continued accumulation of additional profits which serves to enrich all members of the community by the development of new products, jobs and increased payment of taxes to increase governmental activities. This, in turn, leads to more individuals to corrupt and thence to more good.

Bribery, on the other hand, bears the connotation of evil. It invariably involves a selfish act, benefiting no one but the briber, and to a small extent the bribee, which in turn makes turning the briber down or turning him in so much easier.

Now we must be careful to clarify some things about the social order to avoid confusion. One is not classified solely according to his or her paycheck. For example, if one offers money to a sanitation officer who has just cited him for leaving his garbage can uncovered, that is a bribe and should be condemned. It doesn't matter if the offender is a business man, a dentist, schoolteacher, and so forth, since the inspector represents a higher order of society (i.e. sanitation workers in general) and the bribe has nothing to do with the briber's business interests.

Suppose a series of uncovered garbage cans were used to create a smell bad enough to induce certain tenants to vacate an apartment house so it could be razed to construct a new tire factory. If under these conditions a sanitation inspector received a bit of financial help in buying a new house, that is absolutely acceptable, and perhaps even desirable under the circumstances. Think of the widespread use of tires in society, and the number of jobs provided—a staggering advantage over a few tenants who probably wouldn't want to live near a tire factory anyway.

A Force for Good
(A Day in the Life)

Tom Dolan muttered to himself in the locker room as put the final touches on his uniform: "I don't know how I'm gonna tolerate another fucking briefing from that fucking lieutenant." He visualized himself sacking out on one of the back seats at the station house. "That bastard catches me again, he'll have my balls."

"Cut it out, Tom," said Sonny "the Leech". "That cocksucker's got to do something for a living." Sonny was twenty-two years old, dark and handsome, but short. Five feet nine in height with slicked black hair, he contrasted sharply with the six foot three, heavier Dolan. He had been teamed with the more experienced Dolan over the past ten months. They made a good pair. Tom's curses rolled off Sonny easily, and they seemed to take each others criticisms without animosity. Tom lectured incessantly about the evils of the force and Sonny not believing any of that crap, agreed with all the comments.

Actually, Sonny's real name was Salvatore Lichiessani, and "the Leech" stemmed from the fact that no one at the station house could pronounce his name. For three months the men searched for a short nickname and the ideal one presented itself in August of the previous year. Sonny had made a collar on some old drunk who was walking around the neighborhood shops with mirrors taped to his shoes, looking up the dresses of a varied assortment of clerks, secretaries, and housewives when Sonny spotted him. Unfortunately, in applying the handcuffs, Sonny had gotten one cuff caught in the margin of his pants pocket. Not willing to admit his mistake, he brought the guy in by keeping his left leg locked around the prisoner's right thigh. The drunk, of course, was excited by the whole prospect, and it wasn't until Tom Dolan slipped Sonny the key that they got disentangled.

Tom kept his mouth shut and the two became close friends from then on. Of course, the nickname was applied instantly by Benny Lampert, the station's recording sergeant who was thoroughly impressed by the vigilance and determination of the cop in not letting his prisoner have sufficient breathing room. Benny couldn't understand, however, why the drunk kept smiling all through the booking.

Sonny was a native Brooklynite, having grown up in Bensonhurst. He came from a large family—six brothers and sisters. But he was his father's favororite. He was always bright and smiling and as the oldest of the children therefore the peacemaker. He'd dreamed of becoming a cop. When he was eleven years old his father, who owned a 45 automatic, took him shooting.

It was a cloudy drab day when the two of them drove out to Queens. The range was in the basement of a sporting goods store that displayed a wide variety of handguns. The noise, as they entered was deafening, the blasts ringing off the walls of the narrow range. Sonny's father handed him a pair of ear mufflers. There were six slots for shooting and at each there was a broad wooden bar on which the shooters displayed their guns and ammo. A wire ran down the length of each slot on which the paper targets were hung, and then by pulling the wire over a pulley they could be set at a desired distance. The image on the targets was usually some bad guy with circles and numbers outlining his torso. His father taught him respect for handguns, proper management and etiquette. Within a week of their first visit Sonny could take the gun apart, clean and reassemble it.

Local cops would often come to the range to practise. When off duty most could try out a variety of handguns that they collected. Sonny loved the atmosphere and talking to the off duty officers. That clinched it. He was going to be a cop. Assignment to the precinct with Dolan was perfect, a bonus. He determined that going along with the rules of the brotherhood was the road to success and he wasn't going to let anything interfere with his career.

The officers filed out of the locker room and grabbed seats on the scattered wooden folding chairs facing the large district map. Pins of different colors marked the local crime locations reported during the past week. The loud din gradually subsided as lieutenant John Crockett ("the crotch" as labeled by Benny) slowly entered the room. It was clear at once that he was going to have trouble negotiating the short step onto the platform when Benny firmly grasped his elbow and led to the small podium in front of the map.

"Get your fuckin' hands off me, you prick" he muttered as he stumbled up and leaned heavily on the lectern.

"Cocksucker" murmured Tom, and four neighboring cops nodded in agreement.

"I have a major announcement to make to you gentlemen," started Crockett. "We have received a special commendation from the New York Times for the decrease in assault and rape rate in our district. The diligence and hard work of the members of this station house received the notice of the commissioner, and congratulatory notices have been placed in the files of every member of this precinct. Keep up the good work and more commendations will be forthcoming."

"What the fuck is talking about?" whispered John Banks, who had singly brought in four girls the previous night who were victims of a "gang bang" on Fourteenth Street.

Tom turned to him and said, "The idiot lost all the green pins last month. He's been sticking the map with yellow ones. He ain't sayin anything about the embezzlement rate which tripled over the same time. We'll be flooded with those non-uniform types from Central if he keeps up this shit."

Crockett continued "…and the Times is considering offering a special award to the Benefit Fund in our names if we can do the same thing for muggings over the next month."

"Tell Benny to dump the red pins, we'll make a fucking fortune. In fact hide 'em all for a week and we can all take a vacation," said Tom quietly.

Then began a street-by-street outline of the crimes committed during the past twenty-four hours. Two murders on Eighteenth Street, three on Second Avenue, two assaults on Twenty-third Street, a hit and run at Fourteenth Street and Third, three robberies and so forth. By the time Crockett had passed over the map once, he had trouble finding a spot for any additional pins. He turned to face the men. "You gentlemen better move your asses and bring in some of these hoods or the Commissioner is gonna wonder what the fuck you're doin every night."

The men were impressed by the crime wave in their district, and then it came…

"And let me add one little thing. You bastards want to get paid, don't you? Well the city's broke. Last week I passed out a new summons book to every cop and nobody's asked for a replacement. Well you're gonna get one tonight and let me tell you that if your not using it by tomorrow morning you'd better have a good excuse. I'm gonna be out patrolling tonight and if I find one bastard passing a red light who don't have a cop on his tail, there's gonna be hell to pay."

"Shit", muttered Sonny.

"Fuckoff" murmured Tom.

*　　　　　　*　　　　　　*

It was three a.m. Tom and Sonny were parked in an unmarked patrol car with their lights off. Sonny started to doze off when Tom poked him softly with his elbow.

"Look at that. Those bastards have circled the block three times already. Looks like a hit."

Sonny looked up in time to see the late model green Chevy roll around Fourteenth Street and cut on to First Avenue. It was cruising at about fifteen miles per hour, close to the curb. Both men noticed at once that the car slowed passing Feinberg's jewelry store.

"You're right," said Sonny. "It's going to be a fast hit and run for the stuff in the window. Why the hell did Feinberg leave that jewelry in his window tonight? He usually cleans it out."

"He's got that big sale on tomorrow and he wants to get an early start. He usually asks us to watch things when he leaves the jewelry out."

"Schmuck" said Sonny. "It's just there inviting trouble."

*　　　　　　*　　　　　　*

Albert Shawn Goldstein had just turned fifty and was starting a new life. His wife of thirty years had walked out three months earlier and the kids were on their own. He couldn't believe he could enjoy life so much. He was getting laid regularly for the first time, and hadn't had more than four hours sleep in each of the last twelve nights. But he loved every minute of it. And now he had something he'd always wanted to own—a brand new Corvette. He hummed the motor at each traffic light. Listening to the sound made him feel as though he were ready for a part in a major movie. Just breaking it in, he thought, driving twenty miles an hour. Plenty of time to gun it later. He promised himself that he was never going to scratch the paint on this red beauty. It was his, a symbol of a new freedom. He was determined never to clean the front seats, but watch the red, blonde and brunette hairs accumulate on the velour.

He rounded Tenth Street onto First Avenue and headed for his new East Side pad. It was 3:15 a.m.

*   *   *

"Quit poking me with your fucking elbow, for chrissake, I see 'em."

The green Chevy was moving up First Avenue at a slow pace.

"This is it", said Tom, fingering the car keys in the ignition. "We'll pull out and cut 'em off.. You take the car and I'll take the prick that smashes the window. What a shocker!"

The Chevy halted in front of Feinberg's. Only a small streetlight illuminated the area and shadows covered the entrance to the store and most of the street. The silence was broken by a shattering of glass and the shrieking of Feinberg's alarm. At the same moment Tom gunned his ignition and started to move out.

"Did you see that?" yelled Sonny.

"What?" asked Tom.

"That Corvette just went through a yellow light."

"But you're allowed to go through a yellow light."

"Not in a Corvette. Go get him."

"But what about Feinberg's? We got the bastards lined up."

"Fuck 'em, we'll get them some other time. We got a summons book to get rid of."

The unmarked patrol car sped out onto the center of First Avenue turned uptown and headed for the Corvette. Lights were going on in some storefront apartments in response to the window smashing and alarm.

Goldstein couldn't believe what was happening. Two policemen in a car were waving him frantically over to the curb, lights were going on in buildings, somewhere an alarm was ringing. He never saw the overturned garbage pail as he swerved toward the curb, hit the pail, jumped onto the sidewalk and smashed his fender against the fireplug. "Oh my God," said Goldstein, " if those guys are phonies this will be the highest class mugging they've had in this neighborhood in years."

A few minutes later Sonny was speaking to a dazed and traumatized Goldstein: "Albert Shawn Goldstein—where do you think you're going? Traffic lights are meant for the night as well the day." He fingered the license and registration in his hand.

"Officer I was only going twenty miles an hour, The light was yellow, it wasn't red."

"Well sir," said Sonny, " I think you passed a red light and will have to be cited." He started to pull out his violation book.

"Look, can't we do something about this?" Goldstein began to slide his hand into his back pocket, reaching for his wallet. "I don't have any violations, and I don't have time to take care of all this. What do you say."

Sonny looked down at the pale man squirming in front of him. He saw a twenty dollar bill being shoved toward him.

"Are you offering this to forget the ticket?" asked Sonny.

"Look officer, take it if you want it. Let's say it's a donation to the P.A.L."

Goldstein felt Tom's hand firmly grasp his left shoulder. "Okay, sir, that's attempted bribery. You'll have to come down to the station."

"Aw—come on."

Goldstein felt the handcuffs quickly applied and himself forcefully being pulled from the Corvette and seated in the patrol car.

It all seemed like a dream as he heard the policeman murmuring something about his right to contact a lawyer and that anything he said would be held against him, and that the judge would not be in until Monday morning—obviously indicating at least three nights in jail.

"For Christsake", he thought, "I only passed a yellow light."

Tom pulled Sonny aside. "Look Sonny," he said, "take him down and book him and then come back and pick me up on Nineteenth and Second.

"Where are you going?"

"Tonight's the fifth and Harrigan's Bar is two weeks behind on the 'vig'. I'm goin' to pick up some cash for the boys. I'll be in the bar when you get back."

Chapter IV

Corruption In High Places

This chapter illustrates two of the fundamental principles in the use of corruption to facilitate efficient function of the society. It is paramount to realize that no segment of government is immune to its reach, and this is as it should be. Even the most insular segments which appear to function over and above the daily economic strife may be found to be useful under certain circumstances. Remember that the circulation of money stimulates all forms of good. Whenever profits may be realized from a new enterprise there will be associated employment, money to spend, and taxes for the government from which the good and welfare of the society flows.

Unfortunately, it is occasionally true that the immediate effects of cor-ruption may inconvenience a small segment of the population, but it is the overall good of which we are speaking, and the flow of profits will in the long run benefit most of the people. A good example of this second principle is the necessity for unemployment in a democratic society. Although full employment is variously described as three percent unemployment in the views of the most optimistic liberals (never as everybody working) we know that society functions best when the unemployment rate hovers around seven percent.[3] Although on the surface this appears to inconvenience seven out of every hundred able persons, actually it provides greater benefits to all.

This unemployment rate provides a premium core of jobless competing for positions, which guarantees sufficiently low income levels to assure profitable margins for business. This latter effect is, of course, desirable for the continuing successful functioning of a free-enterprise system. The continued development of new goods and services will result in a better standard of living for the majority of people and in addition provides the stimulus which is necessary to enhance the dreams and aspirations of everybody with a television set.

The taxes generated by such a stimulated society provides enough money in unemployment insurance and welfare benefits to those fortunate enough to lack a job, so they can continue to function. They probably make more than they would if fully employed at a low level job commensurate with their experience —if they had to pay taxes. This is borne out by the large number of employables who would rather have unemployment insurance and relax than work anyhow.

In summary, therefore, the two principles are:

---

[3] Harding, W. *How a Society Functions Best* Little Brown & Co. Publishers, 1932 Boston, pp 68-69.

1. No level of government is immune (or should be immune) from corruption.

2. The inconvenience of a few, particularly if temporary, is acceptable in the face of a good profit.

Weathering the Storm

Pete Lorillard was known as a "wheeler dealer" among his associates. Somehow each of his projects had managed to furnish a neat profit, part of which frequently served to stake his next deal. Whether he was into stock transfers, real estate or restaurants made no difference—everything seemed to work to his advantage. His latest ploy was arranging jazz festivals, and the quick profits were huge.

Growing up in the Bronx was no disadvantage. He spent his spare time at the local playground and ballfield. It was an all weather experience with ice skating in the wading pool during the winter and softball during the summer. Pete was given the job of choosing up sides for the games and parlayed this into a huge collection of baseball cards. There were always too many kids who wanted to play, but if you saw Pete privately you could always get a game.

During his high school days he developed a note taking service, the first of its kind in those precomputer days. By convincing a few of the brighter students to make copies of their class notes, Pete found a ready market among the poorer students. College held no interest for him. Money was too easy to come by with simple schemes. He always seemed to find ways to make things work out. A few dollars in the right pocket could usually solve the trickiest problems.

Pete sat quietly in his penthouse office contemplating his latest project. He looked out on a magnificent view of the rivers uniting at the lower corner of Manhattan, flanked by other large office buildings and apartments. He loved twilight best, with twinkling lights beginning to appear in many windows, the large ships docked along the wharves and the silence of the sky threaded with thin wooly clouds variously covering golden segments of the setting sun. The city was quiet at this time in anticipation of a new exciting night alive with restaurants, clubs and discotheques filling slowly with happy people—the livers who knew the best New York had to offer.

He wondered sometimes about his constant drive for success, for money. He couldn't resist a temptation to organize a deal which smelled of success, even if the bad odor it bore was only a faint trace. His mind wandered back to his blue-eyed, blonde high school sweetheart who had jilted him for that fat dental student. No class, he thought, no style. Maybe he'd invite them for a dinner at his private table at Rouge et Noir, the best new French restaurant in New York. Drag her out of her Westchester kitchen so she can see what she'd missed.

His valet stood at the bar preparing a large scotch over ice and a few dry roasted peanuts in a small dish. Pete called him "Cato" after the Green Hornet's sidekick, but his rather muscular frame and Brooklyn accent guaranteed no confusion with the original.

Pete's most recent project had begun to develop in April with a few scattered posters announcing a post summer rock festival. Interest was slow at the start but began to grow with the passing months and further advertisements. He had already banked 450,000 dollars in advance sales with an outlay of 50,000 for the farm, 100,000 for the rock groups, 50000 for promotion and audio, a neat profit of a quarter of a million already, and anticipated continued sales of at least another 3 million. What a snap, he mused.

Cato looked up. "Boss, I'm worried."

"Forget it", replied Pete, "this thing's a snap, can't miss."

"We ain't got no leeway this time. Labor Day's the last day of vacation for most of these kids. If we get rain they ain't goin' to trek out fifty miles to hear some kooky music. It'll kill the last minute ticket sales."

"Cato you worry too much. You know me better than that. It's not going to rain. We're going to have sunshine. SUNSHINE…We'll clear another half million in sales by show time."

"You can't fix God. If it rains the place will be empty. If we don't get a turnout there'll be a demand for rainchecks. That farmer ain't going to give us the place again. It could be a disaster."

"Cato, calm down. Pour yourself a long one and relax. We don't have to fix God. As long as noone thinks it's going to rain the ticket sales will be great—and non refundable."

Pete leaned back in the leather recliner he used for a desk chair. He let his feet rise slowly so he could savor complete relaxation. His fingers closed gracefully around the icy glass as he sipped the cool scotch. He gazed out on the city below, the warm glow of evening descending by stories down the concrete giants lining the river.

What a town, he thought.

$$* \qquad\qquad * \qquad\qquad *$$

Sunday, September 6:

Louis Johnstone entered the long paneled office on the ninety-eighth floor of the Trade Center, shook his umbrella, unhooked his rubbers, quietly removed them and sat down at the head of the long polished oak table. What an awful weekend, he thought.

He glanced slowly around the dark paneled walls covered with maps and charts. The large gleaming barometer sat encased in a crystal cage near the door. "Already dropped a full inch since yesterday."

The door opened and in twos and threes the other members of the panel filed in, took their seats and began intimate conversations in soft rhythmic tones. Four soft bells tinkled and brought the group to attention.

Johnstone waited a moment, fingering the white formal papers before him, assuring absolute silence. He began to read calmly, gathering a certain rhythm as he became more animated.

"Gentlemen, things look bad for tomorrow. There's a heavy low-pressure area moving in advance of Hurricane Filomena "who on earth selected that name," he thought, "with winds increasing to forty knots by the morning. The barometer is at twenty-nine inches and still falling. Weather stations in the Carolinas and South Jersey have reported heavy rains heading our way with gale-force winds. Two ships off the coast are foundering at the periphery of the storm but there's no sign of it heading out to sea. We're in for it."

He glanced at the stiff white bloused Vassar graduate who was taking notes, rose from his chair and turned to the large curtain behind him. With a flourish of his arm he grasped and pulled at the long cord. The heavy curtains parted revealing a huge picture window facing the bay. Splattering droplets danced against the pane, leaving long trails of minute rivulets on the glass.

"Okay I suggest we move ahead to the final prediction for tomorrow. I would suspect that a lot of picnics may be disrupted. May we have a show of hands?—How many of you think it's going to rain tomorrow?"

Johnstone's hand shot up into the air as he looked down the long table…The other nine men sat motionless, no one moving, no one talking.

"Perhaps I wasn't quite clear. We must vote now. Look at the window! We had it installed to improve our forecasts. Use it by God! What the hell do you think is going on? You think the American eagle is up there pissing on us?" Johnstone was flushed with anger. He realized he had descended to a level of conversation which ill befitted a Harvard graduate. But the change in his demeanor was engendered by the sight of his motionless peers and was too difficult to control. Quietly he calmed himself, composure slowly returning, he faced the group.

"Gentlemen, perhaps another vote is in order. Those believing that it will rain tomorrow please raise your hands." He peered at each stony face in sequence.

"Put your hand down, Bess, your vote doesn't count." Again he was embarrassed by the deadly silence—the motionless men avoiding his searing glances.

"Okay, okay," he said finally. "Bess you will report that the weather bureau predicts a ten percent chance of rain for tomorrow."

Sweat beaded his forehead. He tried to calm himself, slowly glaring at the figures along the table. "Gentlemen the meeting is over and I want to thank you for your efforts today. And it is my fervent hope that you may all promptly go fuck yourselves."

*   *   *

Monday, September 7:

Henry Gallagher couldn't believe what was happening. Since he had become sheriff of Woodbridge he had led a calm life, an occasional drunk driver being his most exciting experience. But now this.

He wiped the mud from his shin as he extracted his feet from the soft earth. Before him stretched tens of thousands of young boys and girls, shivering in rhythm to the beating rock music blearing from the loud-speakers, but mostly seeking cover under blankets, dresses, anything that could protect them from the pelting rain. Streams of mud poured down every rise of the farm and lodged in soft pools around the listeners. Loud cheers went up with every new beat, huge claps of static blasted out with every spasm of lightning.

With screams and cries people were looking everywhere for cover, but the farm was almost barren of buildings. Six hundred boys and girls, having read somewhere that intercourse could keep one from freezing to death, were for the first time in their lives applying book knowledge to a real life situation.

"Hank, where'd they all come from? I thought the rain would wash this thing out."

Henry saw his deputy Sam Martin plodding ungracefully through the muck toward him. "They started piling in last night. That blasted weather report predicted only a ten percent chance of rain today. Those bastards must be blind as well as stupid."

"There's a riot of four hundred kids over in the east meadow. They can't keep their joints lit in the rain."

"Let 'em riot. I can't even get anybody mobilized to cover the center area. This is impossible—the temporary toilets won't flush and all the roads are out."

Just then Bob Markham a second deputy flashed a signal in his walkie talkie. "Hank, I'm over near the center stage. The Scuba Tuba won't go on."

"What? What the hell's the Scuba Tuba?"

"Some rock group. They claim they got five inches of rain in their instruments and can't get it out fast enough."

"Just keep someone playing, damn it! If they don't keep playing there'll be a riot."

A loud shriek went up from the left. Hank snapped his communicator on. "George, George, come in. What the hell is going on out there?"

"They're water skiing."

"What? What the heck are you talking about? There's no water."

"That's what you think. Some kids got water skis and they're skiing down the hill in the mud. They're cheering every time someone makes it to the bottom. We got two broken ankles over here already."

The music crackled through the loudspeakers as the winds began to rise. Streaks of lightning flashed through the sky. Henry grasped the door of his patrol car and fingered the inside panel. "Maude—get me the state police on the radio."

"Hello, hello. This is Henry Gallagher at Woodbridge. We're gonna have a riot here soon. This jazz thing's been going on for four hours and the storm's increasing. Hello?"

"PY-51 state police office. Will contact patrol units and report. Over"

"Listen, you guys have got to get us out of this. We've got thousands of cars and kids piled up here half stoned. We've got to clear the area. What's the story on the roads? Can we get them out?"

"PY-51 negative, over."

"What the hell you mean negative? With all the beer we got flowing up here they're gonna change the name of this town to Piss River in another hour."

"PY-51. The roads are blocked by the marchers heading your way. The highway's blockaded. Must be thousands. We can't move anything. Over."

"Marchers? What marchers?"

"PY-51. I'm not sure—they're women—thousands of women—carrying signs reading 'HADASSSAH'—and they claim they're delivering eight thousand umbrellas to your area.

*　　　　　　*　　　　　　*

The clean white schooner clipped its way through the foaming ripples on the calm sea. Pete Lorillard lay contented on the deck on his cushioned contour chaise.

His mind cleared—and rode silently with the rolling waves-up and over, up and over. He reached gently toward the neighboring lounge and ran his hand over the long soft hair—down the curved smooth spine and stopped for a moment on the rounded buttock of the beautiful young lady lying alongside him. He felt the tender squeeze on his arm.

He looked at the crystal sky—not a cloud anywhere—and felt the gentle heat of the sun enveloping him—first his feet, then his legs, abdomen, chest, neck—like a warm furry blanket. He lay back and sighed. With all this, he thought, who needs money!

Chapter V

Clean Government

There is a paradox in our society. Government must serve the needs of the people and to do so effectively it must necessarily lend itself to extensive corruption. Yet exposure of such activity inevitably leads to dismissal of those responsible. Everyone recognizes the existence of corrupt politicians, and if one has a proper sense of sophistication the need for such individuals is eminently clear. We accept them as necessary to maintain our well being in a stable or expanding society. Secretly one may yearn to be a participant in similar schemes so he may also make a "killing" and share in the appropriate rewards.

The average citizen would not likely refuse to accept some inside tip which might yield significant monetary benefits, with the excuse that it wasn't right or fair. On the contrary, most everybody is looking for a route which may lead to a fast bundle. In this sense the small businessman is no different from the corporation CEO, only the scale of the corruption is different. The smaller efforts increase the chances of being caught. Indeed, as we shall note later, there is a general principle that the grander the scheme the lower is the risk of exposure.

Why is it then that indignation rages at the revelation that some political figure has just been caught with his finger in the public till? As any decent psychiatrist can tell us, there are only two factors that lead to all aberrant behavior: insecurity and guilt. (Imagine what would happen to psychiatric fees if they spilled the beans on that one.)

How does one feel when discovering that a high officer of the state has just been exposed as a first—degree corruptor in some scheme or other? The actual behavior of this person in committing the act is not under consideration, and in fact may be the subject of extensive admiration. The problem is that the individual was stupid enough to be caught. After all, can one trust the defense and security of the nation to someone that dumb —(insecurity). And, after all, who was responsible for putting the dummy into office in the first place—(guilt). So, in order to avoid the sense of insecurity and guilt associated with the unfortunate official, the public must resort to the aberrant act of throwing the blaggard out. Hopefully he will be replaced by someone more adept at handling such activity without the consequences of exposure.

One may therefore ask why, if everything that such a person has done is acceptable to the community, should he be exposed at all? Wouldn't it be better in these cases to merely look the other way? To understand this problem we must discuss briefly the function of the press in our society.

There has been an inordinate preoccupation among the American populace in the recent years, with the activities of the security agencies: the F.B.I. and the CIA In fact what people do not realize is that free societies have built into their framework a super security agency—the press. It is the primary function of the pess to expose dummies in office and therefore provide the first line of defense of the nation. Our wise founding fathers knew that a country could not be entrusted to men foolish enough to reveal their corrupt acts, and devised this mechanism to eradicate such nincompoops.

The press has taken up the fight with resounding effect and considerable rewards (do you realize what an advertising page in the New York Times costs?). And the most successful papers are those that have the largest numbers of exposes. Investigative reporters never waste their time on the purveyors of prostitution or dope, but rather on who owns the buildings where these activities are carried on.

How is the government man to protect himself? Well the system insures that only the finest and most long—standing corruptors will reach high office. These, after all, are those most capable persons who may be thoroughly trusted with the reins of government and consequently the lives of its people. Such a person must have the attributes necessary to insure a successful career—ruthlessness, deviousness, unfailing flexibility (or the ability to swim with the tide), and a total lack of any predictable code of behavior. He must, however, use every means to discourage people from believing that he is a perpetrator of corruption and so must adopt an outward appearance totally opposite to his real nature: compassion, honesty, strict adherence to a moral code of behavior, and an unswerving passion to provide a better deal for his constituents. To those who aspire to such positions of responsibility (and profit) I will outline the credo of the government man, which, of course, they all live by:

1. Promise everything.
2. Never put anything in writing
3. Stay out of the newspapers.

The Retaliatory Effort

Joe Reede was mayor of Greenleaf, Colorado. He had been driven to seek office eight years earlier by an inordinate desire to sleep with Mollie LaRue, the waitress in Sam's Take Out Restaurant. Apparently Mollie had been making it with a fair variety of the town's men, but not with Joe. He figured that a prestigious title might change his luck. It didn't.

He had won office in a run-off election with a plurality of thirty votes. The original election had ended in a one—to—one tie and it took an investment of four kegs of beer and free transportation to the improvised election booth to muster the thirty hardy souls necessary to insure a victory. Now he spent most of his time trying to figure out what a mayor was supposed to do.

Greenleaf, situated in the heartland of the Rockies, might have been considered ludicrously as a small town, with the downtown area consisting of Joe's hardware store, a general store, Sam's restaurant and an old filling station. Anyone found driving toward the downtown area was invariably heading for the spur connecting to the main highway. Joe considered, at one time, installing a "one way" sign on that road in deference to the direction that most everyone who used it was taking. An exit sign probably would do just as well, he had thought.

Activity centered around the small outlying farms which supplied most of the food people needed, and enough work for the townspeople. Surrounded by high picturesque mountains, television reception was impossible and amusement consisted of a few scattered radio programs for daily news and the key to the upstairs room at Sam's, occupied by Mollie.

An occasional truck lumbered into town and delivered the few necessities for day to day existence, and picked up the produce and beef to be sold for cash at the markets in towns down the highway.

It was spring, and in Colorado that meant clear, cloudless days, warming gradually under the shadows of the snow—capped peaks. On such a day Joe was seated in his usual position in front of the hardware store. His eyes were half closed against the sun. He glanced sideways towards Tom Marshall, who was running toward him.

"Joe, Joe. There's a fella over at Sam's looking for the mayor."

"Well for christsakes, Tom, don't anyone know who that is? Bring him on down here."

Joe couldn't believe that after all these years he was going to have something official to do. Most folks didn't call him mayor since they were concerned that the title might stimulate some activity,—and no one could predict how that might end up.

The tall stranger walked slowly up the dirt path to Joe's store. He was in uniform and appeared stiff and portly.

"Colonel Edward Syms," he introduced himself, "representing the Department of Defense. Are you the mayor of Greenleaf?"

Joe concentrated on the newcomer. Shiny shoes and buttons, heavy chest (football player?) precise movement, a real tough officer. Must be hell working in his outfit. His glance fell toward the few patches of weeds on either side of the path. Ought to plant some grass, he thought. Looks kind of worn out.

"Yes, sir," answered Joe, who was not sure if mayors got up when they met strangers or just leaned back and waited.

"Pleasure to meet you, sir," said Syms. "Would it be appropriate if we met in your office?"

Joe was embarrassed. Maybe he ought to get himself an office. He saw immediately the possibility that it might do the trick to improve his relationship with Mollie.

"No, this is jes' fine," he said finally "Go on and pull up a chair and let me know what's on your mind."

"Well, we wrote you some months ago, but didn't realize the problems with postal delivery in this area."

Joe hadn't checked for a letter in the past six years, when it occurred to him that he didn't know anybody outside of Greenleaf.

Syms continued. "The Department of Defense has completed a survey of the central U.S. retaliation effort and we have selected Greenleaf as the proposed site for the development of a new missile silo, which will beef up the entire U.S. defense effort. With the decreased likelihood of a major international problem we are concentrating on a few key areas for defense."

Joe was really impressed by now, although he wasn't sure quite why.

"Of course we will build this with all work sponsored and paid for by the U.S. government. The site selected will be five miles north of town at the base of Whittier Mountain. All due effort will be made to cause as little disruption as possible to the town."

Joe sat open-mouth at the whole prospect. "What can I do for you, colonel?"

"Nothing. Nothing at all. Just consider this for your own information, mayor. All the property rights have been secured, of course. And one thing, since the site will be high priority and secret, it will be necessary to disguise the area. I wouldn't want the townspeople surprised by its outward appearance."

As soon as Syms left Joe bolted down to Sam's where Tim Gantry and Ed Smith were sitting and gabbing about the new plantings for the year.

"Hey fellas," he said, "I just got visited by a U.S. colonel."

"No sheeet," said Tim, "what the hell'd he want?"

"Well it seems like the government's gonna put up one o' them missile silos just outside a town," answered Joe.

"Hey," said Ed, "ain't that gonna be kinda dangerous. Those things explode?"

"Naw," chimed in Tim, " they're built pretty solid. Lotta stone and concrete. Mostly underground."

Sam perked up at the conversation. "Suppose them Russians send one of their missiles over here. Ain't they goin' to aim for us?"

"Hadn't thought about that." answered Joe.

The following week trucks, and uniformed men, all bearing the insignia of the U.S. Corps of Engineers created a steady stream of traffic through town and northward. A bivouac area had been set up as construction began with a deep excavation, followed by steel piles, concrete and wooden frames. Gasoline sales at the filling station soared to a hundred gallons a week as each day the predominant activity consisted of driving out to the construction site and observing the progress.

Joe, however, stayed at the hardware store waiting for an official duty to appear, and got most of his information in daily reports from Tom Marshall. Soldiers seemed to mill around in the evening drinking beer and joking with the folks of the town. Joe was a bit uneasy about the fact that Mollie appeared to be losing an inordinate amount of weight and was reassured only by the fact that she smiled incessantly all through the days.

Joe, was in constant touch with the townspeople. Each day the farmers strolled into town and conversations started up about the risks to the town. Joe was concerned. There was a feeling that maybe some action needed to be taken. Some of the folks wanted to contact Washington and maybe stop this thing. Joe needed to take a leadership role to avoid being blamed for any problems that may arise.

He worried about this constantly and tried to figure out a way to get off the hook if things turned out badly. He knew the character of these people. Fiercely independent, and loyal to the U.S., they would support him if he could bring them together on this issue.

Joe called for a meeting of the townspeople. Syms was invited to speak. On a Thursday night in mid March about sixty people gathered at the garage. It was a reletively warm night for this part of the country, although a heavy sweater or jacket was necessary to avoid a chill.

Joe opened the meeting by repeating most of what everybody knew. Syms got up to speak. The crowd was impressed with the variety of ribbons he wore. Clearly he was a veteran of a number of campagnes. Several sons of the towns people were killed in Vietnam, for which they felt proud rather than regretful.

Syms opened with a summary of how the deterrent quality of the missile program had insured the maintenance of peace. He explained how unlikely they were to be attacked. He played on their loyalty and the greatness of America.

Rob Peters, a farmer, arose to question the need for additional missiles. "Ain't we got enough of them already?" he asked.

Syms rose to his feet. "We've got small time enemies all over the world mostly Arabs. They could develop the capability to launch one at us. But they're afraid we might strike back."

Nobody in the crowd had ever met an Arab, much less knew anything about them. They were clearly not Christian, and thus open to suspicion. "I think we got to support the government on this one," said Ed Smith.

There was a patriotic fervor slowly developing in the crowd. Supporting America against the Arabs seemed about as close to God as anyone could get. Occasional comments arose about why Greenleaf was chosen, and the liklihood of some small country getting long range missiles, but the sentiment for allowing the project to continue was overwhelming.

Joe was masterful at his ability to control things and allow this feeling to develop. The people felt that they trusted him, and he wouldn't let them down.

"Joe," said Tom a few days after the meeting, "I can understand the fact that they got to build that place to disguise the missiles. They're putting in a lot of rooms, but I don't understand something."

"What's that?" asked Joe.

"Well, they got a whole unit putting in plumbing and such. I know they's gonna need that for offices and such."

"Yes," said Joe.

"Well, I don' understand why each of them offices has got to have its own bath and shower."

As the weeks rolled by the days became warmer and more pleasant. Yellow buttercups appeared and waved gently in the green meadows. Long furrows, in straight lines covered fields that had lain fallow the year before. An occasional tractor hummed across a field and disappeared behind a frame house, followed by a host of crows that dived and then shied away from the specially treated seed.

North of town the silo began to take shape with its convex windows, rustic outer appearance, and freshly sodded lawns.

Tom Marshall's reports began to come in twice a day as the rate of progress increased.

"Joe, there must be some important brass that's gonna be stationed here! You know they got carpets all over that place. And you ought to see the meeting room. It's gonna be the best lit meeting room you ever seen."

"Best lit?" asked Joe.

"Yeah. They just moved a big crate in. I thought it was a missile. I was scared till I saw the sign on the side. I thought it would be 'danger—explosives' but it just said 'fragile—handle with care'. Ed Conlan's kid pried a plank off the crate and damned if it weren't the biggest crystal chandelier you ever seen."

"Tom have you noticed anything like missiles being moved in? I mean they ought to be arriving by now."

"Oh no," said Tom, "but they put in the missile storage area. What a job. It's all concrete sunk into the ground and surrounded by a flagstone walk. Only on strange thing, though. The floor's crooked."

"What?" said Joe.

"Yeah, it starts up high at one end and slants down so it's real low on the other."

Joe began to wonder about what was going on. "Do they have a drainage area in the center of it?"

"Yeah", said Tom. "I asked them about that but they said it was to protect the missiles if it rained."

Joe was uncomfortable. Too many unanswered questions. As July approached the progress had been phenomenal.

Longer, hotter days occasionally dampened and cooled by a fine sprinkling shower failed to slow the activity at the base of Whittier Mountain. Lights began to appear at night from inside the buildings (there were three now) and worked progressed until late at night. Joe was unaware that men could work in so organized and dedicated a fashion. But he began to wonder at certain inconsistencies. Why did they need to disguise an area that everyone in town knew about? And how were they going to fire missiles from the base of a mountain? And, at whom?

It was Tuesday morning when Tom was reporting that Joe decided he'd better get out to the site and see what was going on.

"They got the strangest thing they just put in."

"What's that Tom?"

"Well, they put this here rope on a pulley up along the mountain. Claim they're gonna use it to haul supplies to the top. What the hell they need that for? What're they gonna do with supplies on top of a mountain?"

The ride out was rough and Joe was filled with doubts and premonitions. Out past Don White's farm circling toward the main road, a freshly paved crossroad had appeared leading toward Whittier. They drove through a large iron gate and onto manicured lawns. Joe faced the missile silo and was stricken by the appearance of its graceful lines, rustic contours, freshly painted windows, large walk and gardens. Tom pointed out the rope and pulleys far to the left.

"Jerk," said Joe. "That's a goddamn ski tow. Call some of the boys together and meet me at the store at one o'clock."

*   *   *

It was nighttime at the communications network at the base of Whittier Mountain.

A voice whispered into a secure phone line: " Hello, hello. This is Syms. Is the senator there? Yes, hello."

The senator answered, "Everything okay, Ed? The brochures are out. The first ones will be arriving in time for the fall skiing. Have there been any inquiries as to the location of the engineers?"

"Taken care of. The records show the units out on maneuvers for four months. We kept everything right on schedule."

"How about the men?" asked the senator. "Will they keep quiet?"

Syms replied, "Sure, they think it's a rest home for psychotic sergeants with T.B. They all want it, and hope they'll never use it."

"Great, Ed," said the senator.

"One problem senator. This guy Joe Reede may be acting up."

"What makes you think so?"

"Well," answered Syms ,"he went and nominated a city council, and to boot , they just sent to Denver for five books on how to pass a law."

There was a silent period then the senator responded "Okay, okay, get hold of this Reede. Tell him he's a partner,—in for ten percent."

Chapter VI

Levels Of Society

We have examined in this book a number of governmental activities pointing out the value of corruption. It is evident that all facets of daily life may be improved through its use. Examples vary, but usually we have directed our thoughts in most cases to effects on people we might meet in our day-to-day contacts. Ranging from local business enterprises to one's home, corruption touches us all, and improves things in clearly tangible ways.

One point I have made is that the corruptor must be of a higher social standing than the one who is corrupted. This leads to the conclusion that there should be a class where corruption may be carried out on a grand scale while the individual members remain incorruptible. In fact, these lions of society will look with disdain upon the menial acts of of corruption that rob the average person of hours of sleep nightly. They are expected to use their power to forge the activities that are the basis of the democratic system. Recognized as fundamental to the framework of society they remain untouchable for their acts. Even if some scheme should turn out badly, they are excused or bailed out merely on the basis of their potential for further corruption.

If a motto could be designed for this group it would be "Think Big". But a motto is unnecessary since the members of this group could hardly behave in any other way.

Huge amounts of money or property are involved in each of their daily transactions so as to boggle the mind of the average citizen. Actually, the grander the scale of the corrupt act, the less likely they are to be found out—since few can imagine that anyone could be that corrupt.

This class represents the fundamental fabric of the democratic society, from which foods, services and money flow in such amounts that the little shaved off the top is barely noticed. And this serves only to make them stronger.

There is no criticism of this group since they control the means of communication and therefore public opinion. They can create one hundred thousand jobs over a cocktail, provide heating oil or light for the entire Northeast over lunch, and dictate the flow of money and interest rates over dessert.

There is a natural aspiration in a free society to climb to the next social stratum. This upward movement is designed to insure additional opportunities for corrupt acts and therefore a more important role in daily life. As each successive level is reached one attains more power.

If a definition of a free society is desired, it might be: a society which permits individual ascendancy up the ladder of social levels. Of course, there is a limit! If everyone belonged to the highest level there would be no levels at all. The only advantage in ascending at all is that there will be someone in the levels below over whom you may exert some influence.

Therefore it is also a general rule that while nearly all individuals aspire to improve their social status, only a few may be allowed to actually make it.

But much of the excitement is in the battle itself. The creation of wealth and opportunity to corrupt is fundamental to the well being of the free society. Education, special training and hard work form the backbone of the moral code of free men so that one day they may be in a position to kick someone else in the pants.

There lies the fundamental difference between the class and classless societies. These latter are represented by restrictive policies that prevent movement between the rulers and ruled and while not strictly classless they are characterized by ambitionless men and women with no chance to laud it over anybody—and therefore no opportunity to improve their lot. What a drudge life is for them—merely eating, sleeping, screwing and watching television.

Compare this to the daily excitement of planning a scheme and getting a bit of action started which may put you on an equal level with the fellow who's been screwing you all these years. The opportunity is there. And high above is the ultimate goal—maybe not in your lifetime but perhaps in your grandchild's—of entering the realm of those lords of society to whom all is available, who wield immeasurable power, and who dispense masses of corruption to make everything better for everybody.

The Club

In the sixties between, Lexington and Park Avenues stood a brownstone building of unpretentious appearance, identified only by a small brass plaque bearing the image of a bird in flight. As one ascended the seven stone steps to the entrance, a small bell could be seen immediately above the plaque.

The door was painted black, which coincided well with the decor of the remaining buildings on the block, and the upper half consisted of a frosted glass pane curtained in white damask. But this was not a private residence.

The greeting upon entering was administered by an elderly gentleman with a large shock of white hair. Dressed in a long-sleeved white, silk shirt, pin striped vest and trousers, one was ushered into a small foyer facing a closed elevator. One was always greeted by name, for the members of this club were well known and made to feel at home.

To the left of the elevator was a solid mahogany half table on which stood a green urn patterned after the Chinese metalware manufactured in a small factory outside London over two hundred years earlier. Anyone caught fingering or examining this antique piece was immediately escorted back out into the street, for the decorum of the club called for total and complete nonchalance in the presence of wealth.

Upstairs the atmosphere was somewhat less austere in the large, mahogany paneled library with its scattered, overstuffed chairs and portraits of famous men—all of whom were members of the club. The room was always quiet regardless of the number of occupants, and conversations could be held in the strictest of confidence that no one was or would want to be listening in. Without a fuss, one's favorite pre-dinner cocktail or sherry, or post-dinner brandy, appeared at his side as if by the machinations of a mysterious force, since the waiters seemed to be invisible.

Guests were permitted, within reason, and would hover about their host in small groups, usually satisfying the culmination of some important deal or transaction.

Generally one could distinguish the guests from their hosts with ease by noting the uniform dress code to which the members adhered by tradition. Utter disregard for style was paramount, for each member was appreciated as a man of proper breeding and background and not for his choice of tailor. This was constantly emphasized by wearing an out-of-date suit, black or gray, narrow lapels, and dark, narrow ties on a solid white or blue background. One would never believe that a particular suit was inexpensive, since personal tailors were required to construct them so they were shiny, out of style with slightly baggy pants, and bearing a constant wrinkle. One member created a sensation by purchasing several suits having a slight tear in the lining, leaving a bit hanging from the bottom of his jacket. He was so greatly admired that he was elevated at once to membership secretary, a post of purely symbolic significance, since all new members had to be approved unanimously in any case.

Women were not permitted since Mrs. Harris Ekkar wore a low-cut black dress, displaying a bit too much and resulting in the spillage of several glasses of vintage port . Lost money, friends, and positions could be easily reacquired, but not vintage port.

Overseeing the nightly activities was the most senior of the members, John Hayes Randolph III. Considered the dean of American finance, he had delved into all aspects of business with success following success, and increased his modest inheritance of sixty million by at least three zeros. So respected, in fact, was JH that his personal recommendation was required for any consideration for membership to the club.

This fact created a mild sensation when JH approved the admission of Daniel Greene, a Brooklyn-born son of immigrant parents who had amassed a fortune dealing in Swiss Gold shares. "Don't worry," JH assured the members, "it's important to let one of them in so we're not labeled as bigoted. Besides, who's he going to talk to?"

JH had suffered unmercifully from prostatism for several years which led to the much celebrated installation of a direct line ticker next to his private urinal. This was the result of a forty-thousand dollar paper loss suffered during one of his frequent visits to the john. As a matter of fact, during a similar episode, the rush to sell led to his urinating a considerable amount down his right pant leg and only the quick wit and resourcefulness of his valet Clarence avoided significant embarrassment.

When JH had a cocktail, it was cocktail time; and when JH went to dine, it was dinner time; and when JH retired to the library after dinner it was clear that dinner was over.

The dining room was elegant, fully staffed by maids and waiters in white gloves and starched uniforms. There was no menu. The members who frequented the finest restaurants the world had to offer, who knew the greatest chefs by first name, reserved for the club those meals which reflected their deepest desires and tastes—things which could not be ordered elsewhere.

On a certain night in August, Earl Homer Collingworth sat at a corner table inhaling the fragrance of a Mouton Rothschild Cadet '74 poured from a crystal decanter. On a silver platter before him lay a thick slab of white bread covered with his favorite loganberry jam and spread thickly with peanut butter. Centering a second piece of white bread over the first he lifted the sandwich to his mouth and savored the elegance of the meal he loved the most.

Suspicion centered about Todd Haynes Eckhardt III when he first ordered his Nova Scotia salmon to be served with cream cheese on a toasted bagel. He explained, however, as he washed it down with a smokey Puilly Fume '71 that it reminded him of his college days when he had made it regularly with a dark haired Jewish beauty from Milwaukee. She , of course, had fantasized the elegance of life as part of a first line family, but he had already promised himself to Abby Clogwell, whom he later married and with whom he sired three of the dullest children he'd ever met.

On this particular night, JH sat at his private table, near the toilet, when he noticed the eye signals directed at him by Harwood Cline Schiller. Randolph was on his second bowl of cornflakes and milk when he decided that it was best to acknowledge something was up.

Harwood approached his table cautiously. "JH, I've got to solve a fairly touchy problem."

"Related to the railroad?"

"Yes," said Harwood. " we may be going down the drain and I need your advice."

"After dinner in the lounge.—After dinner, "said JH wiping a small drop of milk from the corner of his mouth and signaling for another dish of raisins.

"By all means," said Harwood, and returned to his Cheval Blanc '55, sipped it softly and dipped his long spoon casually into the bowl of franks and beans sitting before him.

Alvin Harcourt at a neighboring table noticed the conversation and put down his chilli burger long enough to slip a sly wink at JH. They had discussed Schiller's problem before, and knew that before long there would be money to be made.

Dinner was usually finished by nine and was especially prompt tonight as the members singly retired to the lounge to await the game. It was going to be unusually fierce tonight, and the sense of something in the air pervaded the club.

The lounge was paneled as in the other rooms, but carpeted in a thick blue pile with matching drapes, and lit brightly by a central crystal chandelier. The members took their respective places, each sitting on the floor, comfortably cushioned. Small tables bore the ash trays for their cigars as brandy was poured into sparkling snifters. They formed a small circle as the great central board was positioned.

"All right, Harwood, what seems to be the problem?"

"It's the railroad—you know the large hotel we built—we have invested over eighty million in the most fashionable resort. But the weather won't hold up—and the area's wrong. We'd hoped to stimulate rail travel, but it's not going. With recurring losses, the whole railroad might go under."

JH snickered to himself. "Have you started unloading?"

"Yes, we've been buying and selling railroad shares for two months now. We'll end up with twenty million shares unloaded by next month. The price has held so far, but it'll break as soon as our next statement is out."

"You're personally home free then?"

"Yes, but we can't let the railroad fail. A bankruptcy would be too embarrassing. There'd be questions about our investments. After all, the railroad is an American institution."

The game was starting. Out of deference JH handled the dice first. He smiled silently as he reeled them onto the board. A five and a three. "Vermont Avenue," he said, "I'll buy it."

Harwood fidgeted incomfortably and threw a five. "Oh for christsake. Reading Railroad. I don't want it."

"Good, I'll take it," said JH as he signaled to the bank to tally the cost. "Harwood, you should know better. I've told you many times that you can't build hotels on the railroads. You should have stayed with better properties!"

Excitement grew as the yellow, green and orange cards were passed around, all representing real properties. Deals were made, side bets, special arrangements to avoid rental payments.

"Let the stock fall," said JH, "We'll pick it up later. You're not to touch it. By next Tuesday announce the bankruptcy. By Thursday congress will pass special legislation to grant an interest—free loan to this great American institution and place it in receivership. We'll take it over. Blame it on the airlines. You're out—stay out. Be glad you weren't hurt. Harcourt here will be named director by Congress. The president will go along."

"Thank you, thank you JH."

JH waved off the compliment. He stared deliberately around the board. "Now whose got the Pennsylvania," he said.

Chapter VII

Special Relations

The manner in which the corruptor deals with his personal life is an important aspect of the entire operation. There are a few guidelines which should be carefully followed in order to insure as little interference as possible. Since the smooth functioning of the society depend heavily on successful corruption, the corruptor should consider it his patriotic duty to do the thing right.

A. The wife

Primary rule: Never tell your wife anything about your business activities. It is generally a good policy to plead poverty at every available opportunity. This usually serves to improve one's personal relationships, since she will believe that anyone working so hard and earning so little must love her very much.

One close friend and corruptor, for example, drove his Honda from home each day, parking four blocks from his house where he was met by his chauffeur driving his Mercedes 680. This maintained the proper appearance at both ends of the trip, poverty at home and affluence at the office. Be careful that a casual glance by your wife at the mileage doesn't engender suspicions when she wonders how come after two year of owning the family car, you've only driven it twenty miles. Better disconnect the thing altogether.

If your wife is particularly astute, however, she may wonder about your wardrobe of eight-hundred-dollar suits. After all, it would be too inconvenient to change clothes four times a day! This can usually be handled by granting her the use of a new credit card. Wives who can be kept occupied by shopping usually display a remarkable tolerance for any unusual behavior on the part of their husbands.

Speaking of credit cards, there is an obvious circumstance that should be watched for. This is particularly true if the wife pays any of the bills. Carry cash! This avoids considerable difficulty in explaining an American Express charge for Joe's Motel on the other side of town.

In choosing a wife, the astute businessman will pay special attention to her high-school grades, which can be obtained from any guidance counselor for twenty bucks. She's ideal if she failed math, and this can be extremely useful should there be a need for alimony payments at a future date.

B. The Daughter

Daughters are particularly easy to handle. They believe in the honesty and integrity of their fathers under the most humiliating circumstances.

One girl, for example, was convinced that her father was a world renowned brain surgeon in spite of the fact that he was missing three fingers of his right hand.

Doubts can always be dispelled by a few dollars for a new dress. They can be counted on to be the staunchest allies in times of stress.

C. The Son

Sons are a different problem. They are much more variable and unpredictable. One never knows how they will turn out. In general it's probably better to spoil them unmercifully with gifts and toys when they are young, and cars when they are older. Never give them cash since they will usually blow this by flying to California to join a cult.

D. The Mistress

Choosing the proper mistress can be a particularly tacky problem. The first rule is never to pick one on the basis of sexual prowess alone, since this can often be arranged for more cheaply at any good massage parlor— with a hot shower and sauna to boot.

A mistress must be cultivated slowly to be sure that a communication of minds exists that makes the whole thing worthwhile. Never discuss business or sources of income. In fact, it is best if she is convinced that you are a shoe salesman from Detroit.

Under no circumstances must she know any details of your activities in keeping society going. Her wrath will be unbridled if she ever finds out that you really are married.

If she wonders how you can afford the apartment and lovely gifts, just tell her that the shoe business is great this year.

A relationship with one's mistress must be based on mutual understanding, cooperation and vigorous bedtime activities. Never fall into the trap of becoming a "schmuck" which is a quaint term impossible to translate but easy to define:

"Schmuck": A man whose mistress doesn't understand him.

E. The Secretary

She should know everything that is going on, since she may have to handle your affairs while you are in court testifying. The whole relationship must be built on loyalty. This can be engendered if you select a thirty four year old, blue eyed, single, blonde who is convinced that at any moment you are going to leave your wife and marry her. It's easy to establish this relationship since it's what she wants to believe. Just don't do anything to discourage her.

By all means, don't hesitate to invite her to Sunday barbeque where you can criticize your wife for her extravagances and thereby convince your secretary that she would make a far better mate. This will ease your wife's suspicions also, since she will be convinced you would never invite your mistress home. Thus neither of these important women in your life will suspect that on Tuesdays and Thursdays…

F. Uncles Aunts and Cousins

These relations should be kept in the dark about all your business affairs since they would only want a piece of the action. Keep repeating that business is already twenty percent ahead of next year. That will keep them guessing.

The Son-in-Law

George Hines Albertson III paced across the rug that centered his forty-foot living room. He glanced at the elegant furniture, each piece designed from similar models he had seen in museums on his many European trips. Portraits of elderly provincial ladies and gentlemen hung throughout the room. He pretended these were his relatives from colonial America. He had adopted the III after his name when he entered college, on a lark, for no reason, but this immediately led to his being rushed by the best fraternities on campus and led to a rash of popularity lasting the entire four years.

He now lived in a 20,000 square foot house, part of his forty acre estate on the North Shore of Long Island, overlooking the Sound. From the road, passers-by would obtain glimpses of a large stone house through the hedges lining the estate. This was actually the servants' quarters.

Further down the landscaped lawn stood his home, flagstone front, ivy climbing alongside the huge wooden doors. The central hall led to a white circular stairway lined by paintings of horsemen in red and blue uniforms in various equestrian poses, some carrying guns and others with long, thin, metallic trumpets. Tall Irish wolfhounds roamed at the feet of the various stallions.

His wife sat calmly, relaxed in a high-backed Hepplewhite chair staring at the pacing figure before her. She finally looked up, sipped a sherry from a thin crystal goblet.

"George, it won't do any good to pace around that way. We've got to think of something. She's starting to eat more and more. She'll be dowdy in a few more years."

"I know. You're right, of course. I can't bring myself to tell her. She really looks up to me."

"That's part of the problem. She's never been able to find anyone who could match your…charm.

"Don't be snide, Gladys. It's not becoming. She loves me because I'm her father. Isn't there someone she likes? She's been sulking for months. There must be someone responsible for that."

His wife placed her glass gently on a slender side table. "Twenty-six years old," she said, "and she still sulks when she gets a crush on somebody—. Why at her age—"

"Gladys," George cut in, "let's not repeat ancient history. Just make sure it stays ancient."

Mrs. Albertson III lifted her glass, taking another sip, and looked casually around the great room. "I think she likes that fellow, Jim something-or-other at your office. You know, the one that's always pinching the secretaries. What else does he do anyway?"

"He functions, he functions. He has a bright streak, too. College graduate, but a real horse's ass when it comes to women. Are you sure that's who it is?"

"Yes, pretty certain. I mentioned him the other day at lunch and she stalked off crying. I'd say it was pretty certain."

George hesitated a moment, then asked "Where did she meet him?"

"Oh, don't be stupid, George," his wife hissed, "That girl has been up to your office ten times in the last month. You certainly don't think she's that attached to you."

"So that's the reason. I wondered why she's made so many shopping trips to the city. I should have guessed."

"Well if we don't find somebody soon," Gladys continued, "she'll never get married." There was a moment of silence, Gladys rose and faced her husband. "Can you do anything? Surely he must have some attraction to your money,—even if nobody knows where it came from."

"Don't start that again, Gladys. If you need anything just ask."

"You know I don't need anything, except maybe you—once in a while."

"Okay, okay,—I've been very busy."

"Can you do anything?" she repeated.

"We'll see, we'll see."

*   *   *

Jim Dibella sat quietly at his desk, afraid to move, slowly contemplating the swelling against his right thigh as he stared at Velma across the room. Her long red hair hung loosely over her shoulders. She wore a simple peasant blouse, filled by her large breasts, and cut low enough to produce his current arousal.

Gotta stop, he thought. I won't be able to stand up in a minute. What a piece.

He had tried for months to impress her without success. It cost him a fortune to get his hair styled just right, long in front and carefully trimmed in back. He shopped for new clothes that would allow his muscular build to shine through. He threw away all his t-shirts, wore Conoe under his arms everyday—all to no avail. He could not get her to budge.

Must be a lesbian, he thought. But this excited him even more. Christ, I better think of football players again. I can't even make it to the water cooler.

"The boss wants these accounts completed."

Jim's job was account arbitrator. When large shipments of imported condiments were completed to customers Jim then contacted them to assure delivery and payment.

He barely looked at the papers thrust at him. He closed his eyes. Jerry Rice, Jumbo Elliot, Dan Marino. He saw Dan Marino fading back to throw a long one. What the hell was that receiver doing with long red hair. Christ, he thought.

Jim lived in a small, East Side apartment since college. He was ambitious, but found he had a weakness in constantly thinking about the many short-skirted girls surrounding him. He'd scored several times, but usually had a hard time finishing a good play. People, girls, just didn't take him very seriously.

After a light dinner and a change of clothes each night, he would try his luck at one of the local bars. Usually he ended up watching Jay Leno by himself.

On this particular night he found himself more excited than usual. He couldn't get Velma out of his mind, and began to reel off football players to get himself back on track: John Elway, ...Reggie White...Oh my God.

He wandered aimlessly at first and then into Fat Fannie's on Third Avenue. Each bar followed a similar formula. Unusual name, few seats, weird decor, cheap drinks, and hopefully a few gay waiters. The attraction, however, was the crowding at the bar. No one ever seemed to eat anything, but the body contact was ferocious.

Every girl tried to look as though she had just wandered in from Ohio, by mistake, and the men as though they were auditioning for a role as an adagio dancer—open shirt, casual hairdo, something metal hanging around their necks.

Jim stood at the bar looking over the field. Where to start, where to start? He fingered his shirtfront. His medallion kept slipping into his shirt. He knew it had to show. He couldn't get the collar to lie straight. Every time he opened another button, the collar curled. This bothered him, but not as much as his lack of thoracic hair. He'd thought about going for a hair transplant on his chest, but couldn't find anyone that would do it. He opened the next button and the disc flew out and hung loosely. He straightened his collar and looked around.

It was almost a full minute before he could believe his eyes. She stood at the other end of the bar, still wearing the low cut white blouse, but now with tight black pants outlining her soft round buttocks. He noticed the outline of her thigh, firm and full.

"Velma," he said. He painfully edged his way through the crowd, trying to whip his medallion from side to side for effect as he moved. He felt the back of a small blonde girl as he moved along. "I'm from Canton," she said as she turned around.

"Velma," he said again, " I can't believe it. What are you doing here?"

"Hi Jim." she smiled, her long hair flowing loosely as she turned. "Why I just thought I'd stop in for a drink."

"Let me buy it for you," he said as he turned to the bartender. She ordered a scotch sour. Jim thought a moment and then ordered a Tanqueray martini, which was the most sophisticated drink he could think of at the moment. He forgot the twist of lemon.

"Gee, Jim, you look very good tonight."

I don't believe it, he thought, she's not really here.

They spoke quietly for a few moments as each sipped their drink. Jim swaggered slightly as each asked the usual questions concerning Joe Papp's latest play, a new Greek restaurant on second avenue, the inner meaning of a recent article on the Op Ed page of The Times.

Jim noticed the olive sitting in the bottom of his glass. He bit hard on it. The pit was still in. What the hell do you do with an olive pit, he thought.

The crowd at the bar swelled. The decor in Fat Fannie's resembled the living room in an African hut, covered with swinging fake leopard skins, masks, some smiling as though they had just devoured an enemy chieftain, and the odor of the menagerie at Barnum & Bailey's Greatest Show on Earth, which was sprayed in by an atomizer every hour to maintain the proper atmosphere.

The swell at the bar surged and Jim felt a soft breast against his chest. The damned pit, he thought, as he swallowed hard.

Velma touched Jim's hand as the evening drew on. He felt something metallic in his hand as she brushed closely to him. He could smell her perfume. She said goodbye.—he looked down as he opened his fingers. It was a key.

*   *   *

Three weeks had passed when Jim got the invitation. It was simple-dinner at the boss' home. He hadn't seen Velma since that night. It was rumored that she had been promoted to another department.

Jim thought about but couldn't fathom the reason for the invitation. Probably had something to do with his daughter. She was always hanging around. Pudgy kid. No kid, he thought.

He arrived by taxi from the railroad depot. He knew Albertson was rich but he never imagined anything like this. The house—the mansion—was imposing. Must have married money. Surely business wasn't that good.

He was ushered in by the butler. The huge central hall was imposing with its crystal chandelier, circular staircase, and huge doors leading to the library or living room or dining hall. It was truly a hall—mahogany paneled, eighty feet long, huge leather chairs facing the gleaming table set with fine lace and sterling silver.

Cocktails were served by a white-gloved maid and followed shortly by a formal march into dinner. Only the four of them were present. Mr. and Mrs. Albertson and Deirdre. Short, blonde and pudgy.

The conversation was all inconsequential. He reviewed his educational and family history, traded college stories, and a few current event quips. What's it all about, thought Jim. He knew he carried a fair amount of responsibility at the firm, but not enough to warrant this.

After dinner the women disappeared and Jim and Mr. Albertson were left alone in the dining room.

"Jim," said the boss, "come along with me, I've a bit of a surprise I'd like to show you." They walked through the lengthy room and out through a door to another paneled room. The house was quiet as Albertson lifted a key from his pocket and opened still another door.

Jim was surprised as they entered a small movie theater, equipped with cushioned seats, fully draped to protect the sound, with a projection area in the rear.

"My wife and I occasionally entertain here," said Albertson, "but it also has additional uses."

Jim was silent. The whole scene was leading somewhere, but he sensed he'd better just observe for a while and be quiet. They slid calmly into the plush seats.

"Ever go to any of those x rated sex movies?"

"Once in awhile," answered Jim, who was actually embarrassed at the query.

Albertson raised his hand and the lights dimmed gradually. A curtain parted and a large screen slid into place. Jim sat back as the movie started. The name flashed on.

Overexposed Tonsils rated xxx

Jim flushed as the picture ran on. It was a sexy comedy about a poor girl whose neck glands enlarged following each series of certain sexual exploits. She was diagnosed as having cancer when she's saved by a Viennese surgeon who performs a tonsillectomy. The post operative follow up examinations were sensational. Jim remembered the film now. He had heard that the divorce rate among Ear Nose and Throat doctors tripled within three months of the first showing.

Jim was hot and began to sweat throughout the final scenes.

"I don't understand why you're showing these to me," he said.

"Because I make these films."

"You what?"

"I produce them, sell them, market them. It's worth a fortune if handled properly."

"But the business?"

"Just a front. The real money's here. I'm not really English. I'm Italian. Just like you."

"You mean you're the Long Island Porno King?" Jim was incredulous. He had no idea. Now it seemed simpler since he had doubts about the sales of the business producing this kind of wealth.

"I suppose."

"But why tell me all this? And why show this film? I know it's a big seller and all—"

Albertson interrupted, "Oh it's not this film I wanted you to see, Jim. It's the next one."

Jim felt a weakness in his knees as he sunk back. Albertson raised his arm again and the lights dimmed.

The movie flashed on. Without titles this time.

Jim sunk deeper into his seat as the scenes flashed by. His face reddened as he saw Velma, the red hair covering him as he tripped trying to get his left leg out of his pants. Her, falling all over him as he vainly tried to pull his shorts over his pants. The whole scene was comic except for the fact that he was the unwilling agent of the comedy.

"Oh my God," he said, "they got the whole thing."

"That's my next hit, Jim." said Albertson "It'll be a riot."

"You can't."

"Do you want to sue?"

Jim lowered his head further. "What do you want?"

"Jim, I never had a son, and I want one,…by marriage of course. I think with a bit of reflection you'll see the advantages. They could be considerable."

"Why me?"

"Well, Jim you meet the classic requirements. First of all, my daughter likes you. Second, you know enough of my business to become a valuable partner. And third, if I should decide to retire, your first-hand knowledge of the business should make it easy for you to take over."

Jim let his face drop into his hands.

"Fourthly, I am sure you will agree in view of this evening's activities, that I can be assured of a significant amount of loyalty…"

"Oh my God!" said Jim.

"Now, the only thing we have to decide upon, is the date."

Chapter VIII

Contacts And Payoffs

Contacts

For the gentleman in need of a special favor or two, it is important to know where to go. This manual therefore, will provide, as a public service, some simple rules on how to go about setting up such a deal.

It is obvious, for example, that one cannot suddenly appear in the halls of the State Capitol announcing that he is looking for a political fix. Except under very lucky circumstances he is likely to be hauled away and locked up. Newspaper advertising can also be very misleading. An ad calling for a special contact will usually bring a response from some very kookie single girls, which may have some application in a different kind of manual.

No, in all activities involved with corruption it is important to follow strict rules of behavior to avoid the wrath of the incorruptables (see definitions). So the following few notes will clarify the likely methods of making the initial contact and point up some of the pitfalls to avoid.

A. The Taxi Driver

An excellent source. Taxi drivers usually know all aspects of the city life and therefore who to approach for special favors. This is due to a special talent for memorizing all conversations held in the back seat while pretending utter disdain for all humanity. Actually, many taxi drivers have got disdain for all humanity, but this does not impair their hearing.

It is vital to be clear, however, in your request. For example, asking for a fix can lead to an embarrassing experience if the driver happens to be a narc in disguise. One elderly gentleman from the suburbs recently tried to fix a variance he needed to build a circular driveway he'd wanted all his life. He asked the taxi driver for the right contact and ended up spending four days in a plush East Side message parlor. While the experience was not altogether disappointing, he never got his driveway. So be clear.

If the driver who is approached answers: "That's not my job," the safest thing to do is to get out of the cab immediately since it is likely that he doesn't know how to get to your destination either. Hail another cab and try again.

B. A Candy Store Owner who Drives a Cadillac

This can be one of the best sources for lower level favors such as fixing a building inspector,—a highly useful source, especially if the Cadillac is white.

In driving through a neighborhood, look for a candy store with lots of people filing in and out. Since everybody knows that you get cavities from candy, it is likely that something else is going on. This can be confirmed by slapping five dollars on the counter and asking for O. Henry. If the response is "Is that to win?," you're in the right place. Otherwise you will collect a fair number of candy bars (which can be dispensed to annoying nephews in the hope they get tooth decay).

C. Italian Friends

While it is true that the vast majority of Italians are hard-working decent people, they usually can be relied upon to know the best places to get Italian food. Ask one where you can get the best Calimari in town. Chances are you will be directed to a dingy, out-of-the-way restaurant named somebody's-or-other's Clam House. Don't be afraid to walk in, as your chances of getting mugged are considerably lower than being attacked in the Oval Office of the White House. (maybe a questionable analogy?)

Sit down quietly and look for a somewhat paunchy man wearing a dark shirt and a light-colored tie. Pay no attention to the two mugs sitting with him but make your contact by passing him a note via the waiter. Be explicit, however, since it would be a disaster to be misinterpreted under these circumstances.

D. Jewish Friends Who Manufacture Dresses

A particularly bad source unless you are interested in fixing some minor union official or a head waiter. These friends are very useful, however, in arranging trips to Las Vegas.

E. Get a Lawyer

As a last resort, a lawyer will usually know the right contact. This is likely to be quite expensive, since they always cut themselves in for a percentage.

Be careful, because they will always try to tout you on a legal way to circumvent the law you want to by-pass, and in the long run this will end up costing you more money, especially in legal defense fees.

Payoffs

It is clearly understood, but nowhere inscribed, that compensation for a corrupt act is never handled at the time of discussion. Whether reimbursement occurs before or after delivery is immaterial since all parties to the arrangement are honorable persons demonstrating their loyalty to the democratic system by the very act itself.

It is therefore necessary that a system of delivery be devised which is both effective and devious enough to bypass those angels of the masses—the G-men—whose duty it is to give the appearance of constantly apprehending evildoers, while in fact they are frequent participants. They maintain their roles as guardians of the masses by dint of the general ignorance of the average man about the machinations of corruption in keeping things moving properly.

In order to maintain this appearance of guardianship, the police have developed the most sophisticated equipment to detect crime ever devised and are in a constant state of activity involving surveillance and apprehension. Criminals under arrest are photographed, details published in the local press, houses put up for sale or confiscated. The extent of the dealings are multiplied by several thousand to give a grand total of enough magnitude to reassure the public. If any interested party ever thought to inquire as to the fate of these arrested criminals he would find that few, if any, ever make it to jail. Their punishment for being stupid enough to be caught usually involves the payment of large fees to lawyers specializing in avoiding jail sentences for their clients. Needless to say, such firms are eminently successful.[4]

A number of standard methods for payoffs have been designed to confound the authorities. A few of the more common techniques follow:

The Brown Paper Bag

The brown paper bag is a favorite method of carrying large amounts of money. It is a common sight, clearly indicative of poverty since it usually contains two bologna sandwiches and a pickle. One would never think to pile money in an attache case since only important documents such as mortgage foreclosures are carried in such prominent receptacles.

The unobtrusive brown paper bag, therefore, has assumed great prominence as the payoff container. Various methods of passing cash in a prearranged manner have been designed.

Back Seats of Taxis

This favorite method of passing the cash is founded on split—second timing. The payer will take a taxi to a prearranged meeting place (street corner), leave the taxi with the paper bag on the back seat, while the recipient enters through the same door, taking the taxi to his destination.

As mentioned before, the timing must be accurate, particularly in busy cities where much of the action goes on. Recently a recipient was a step behind and an aggressive but unsuspecting young female, seeing an available taxi at last, darted into the back seat and took off, (the driver cursing under his breath at the anticipated poor tip). Somewhat surprised, she screamed at finding the brown paper bag with ten thousand dollars in small bills, which immediately ruined any possibility of stuffing it into her purse and taking off. The poor payer, naturally, had no recourse but to deny that he had ever been in that cab, ever carried paper bags with money, or even knew where to get ten thousand dollars in small bills.

The Tree Stump

Hollow tree stumps in parks were at one time extremely popular dropping-off places. The appropriate designation would be made and the pickups could be accomplished at any convenient time. Coded maps of the best areas were surreptitiously published and passed around when the arrangements were made. The large number of dead trees made surveillance impractical.

---

[4] *Crime and no Punishment ed.* Seagull, B. Plenum Press 1946, Las Vegas.

A small businessman from the Bronx became wealthy by manufacturing plastic tree stumps which closely approximated the real thing. You could buy one with holes at eye level, hip level, or top-sided holes for easy placement of payoff packages. In addition you had the added advantage of moving the payoff spot to any area of town.

Business boomed until an unfortunate event occurred. A huge squirrel, seeing the package placed, darted after it and being somewhat disappointed at not finding a bunch of chestnuts, deposited a large commentary of his disappointment on the surface of the bag. Two hours later a prominent bank vice-president reached down the stump to get the package and was greeted by a most disagreeable experience. When word got around, the taxi business began to pick up again, and the Bronx businessman began to manufacture living room tables.

∗   ∗   ∗

The Right Man

Herman's Delicatessen in Manhattan was a busy place for takeout lunches. Founded during World War II at the height of the meat shortage, it was labeled as a likely site for evildoings. The police were not sure what was going on, but they knew it smelled bad (not the food, of course).

Surveillance had been increased recently by the addition of Lieutenant Joe Ferguson, the top—notch watcher, who was assigned to the restaurant when suspicions were aroused by the hiring of the mayor's son to cut salami. Everybody knew that somehow information relating to cash payoffs were being passed at the Deli—but the exact method couldn't be detected. Furguson was assigned to have lunch at the place every day and make direct notes of all the activities.

Nothing turned up. He wondered if he had been spotted. Impossible—his disguise was perfect: pinstripe suit, attache case, the perfect Jewish banker or insurance salesman. No one would suspect he was an Irish cop. Impossible, he thought as he swallowed another portion of his corned beef sandwich—on white bread with mayo.

Barney Feinstein was a likely suspect. Joe was sure he was the man. Feinstein ran a small newsstand down the street from the Deli, and each day he would come in, pick up a sandwich, and march out. Payment was made on a monthly basis, but each purchase was followed by the usual totaling of the amount on the front of the paper bag. Furguson was sure that this bag contained the information which could blow the operation—perhaps the address of the drop.

Each day Joe watched as Feinstein stepped out of the store to a small park across the way, toss the bag and sandwich wrapper into a nearby trash can and eat his sandwich while sitting on a bench. The routine never changed.

Furguson fingered him as the likely suspect and Feinstein was in for a careful going over. One day on his way back to his newsstand Feinstein looked surprised to see four men scrutinizing the garbage can near his park bench. They turned it over and began to collect garbage in a cloth sack. Weirdos, he thought. The police examined every aspect of Feinstein's sandwich wrapper and brown bag. They looked for coded messages, invisible ink, microdots, anything that might lead them to the payoff spot, but to no avail.

That night Feinstein was mugged for the first time in his life. Nothing was taken, but he was searched and let go. "Odd. They never took my wallet," he later told his wife.

Ferguson was getting more frustrated each time the squad failed to turn anything up. He arranged for a car to ram the newsstand. No one was hurt, but papers were strewn all over the street. Strangely, there were groups of men immediately on the scene helping Feinstein to clean up. They seemed to be looking for something.

Furguson mulled everything over as he finished his sandwich. Feinstein's the man, all right, he thought. I'll get 'im. He got up paid for his lunch, walked to the door, and stepped outside into the gray afternoon. He glanced down the street, breathed a sigh, crumpled up the register receipt for his lunch and tossed it in the gutter. He walked slowly back toward the office.

A few minutes later a window washer who had been standing nearby idled toward the edge of the sidewalk. He bent down and grasped the crumpled receipt, flattened it out and perused the numbers.

Sand	1.44
Tax	3.80
Total	5.24

He deciphered it immediately—144 W. 38th street, the payoff site that day. He placed the paper in a pocket and resumed washing the windows.

Three eighty tax on a sandwich…that's dumb, he thought. They'd better think up something better soon!

Chapter IX

Handling The Taxman

Each society must have its amusements. For those who understand the system, life would be monotonous if it weren't for the occasional challenges that are presented. In order for those who wield power to have fun, a substructure has been created composed of individuals dedicated to bringing down the leaders. Naturally, this is pure nonsense, since success would undermine the society which nurtures these individuals. Definitely self destructive. However, a considerable amount of excitement is engendered by a constant battle—similar to a hunt—which pits the substructure against the superstructure. Laws are passed to provide a set of ground rules carefully worded to avoid any possibility that those in control can lose the game, which is as it should be. But it wouldn't be fun if the prey knew that they were destined to lose. As a result, a cadre of the substructure is developed to act as instigators (the quarry), convinced they are the guardians of the tranquility of day-to-day life, never realizing that they cannot defeat the hunter.

This makes the chase more exciting. The hunters are distinguished by their refusal to use bribery (a cardinal sin), but short of that, it is wide open. Any means to defeat the prey, legal or not, are not only condoned, but are, in the proper circles, lauded.

The victims of this particular game are members of an organization known as the Internal Revenue Service in the U.S., bred especially to believe that they guard the peace, trained in the latest methods of computer technology, never realizing that they must always be one step behind. From time to time small morsels are permitted to be consumed by these agents in order to maintain their vigor during the hunt and to bolster their morale. But, in fact, the valued members of society are barely touched.

On a simple level, legal means are used to thwart the efforts of the IRS by clearly using the wordings of the laws to defend the system. On a higher plane, however, there are those true hunters whose imagination is stimulated by the hunt and who produce a series of extraordinary coups to not only frustrate but to utterly destroy their victims.

To these men the people doff their caps, for not only do they perpetuate the society, but they create an atmosphere of success. They do more than can be expected. They have fun.

Games People Play

John Corcoran had made the grade. Having spent an inordinate number of hours studying for the CPA qualifying examinations, an effort that was rewarded by three sequential failing grades, he had been hired by the Internal Revenue Service. This was the result of a psychological profile which had detected an enormous animosity toward the medical profession, leading to a fifteen—point bonus and immediate placement.

He arrived early the morning of the fifteenth and noted the commotion at the entrance to the building on Fourth Avenue. A police line had been set up and many of the employees of the service were banned from entering. Three police cars and a city ambulance blocked the parking lot and a multitude of onlookers stood by awaiting some sensational development. Corcoran approached the wooden barrier and noticed Phil Burns standing nearby.

"What's up, Phil? Somebody got shot?"

"Wouldn't this crowd just love that! Somebody's girlfriend carried out in handcuffs would guarantee a successful day. I'm not sure, but I heard that they're taking someone out of the building. Ed Foyers thinks somebody went haywire upstairs."

They were standing fifty yards from the front entrance, and through the glass doors they could detect disorganized movement within the marble lobby. Pressure from the surrounding crowd increased as two of New York's finest exited and headed toward a nearby police car.

Although sunshine obliterated a clear view of the interior lobby, John could make out the form of two figures clad in white uniforms dodging through a small crowd of executives. Between them was a tall figure, clearly being directed to the door with force. The figure appeared diminutive beside the burley attendants. John noticed that each attendant seemed to concentrate on one half of the figure, slowly coordinating their movements toward the doors.

"My God," he said, "it's Fairly."

"Ya know, he's been flying low the past two weeks. He's missed the 'chase' for the last eight days and has been hard to understand since Wednesday. He was moping around. Everybody thought he was acting strange."

"Jesus," said Corcoran. "He's a hero. What the hell's going on?"

George Fairly was indeed a hero. He graduated cum laude from a classic program in the arts at Dartmouth. With his future wide open, he decided upon a graduate education in mathematics, which was an overcompensation for having failed arithmetic in public school. He then fell prey to a pretty dark haired girl from Queens in New York City who serviced him regularly and convinced him that immediate marriage and a calculable income were far better than a long string of degrees. George succumbed. His position at IRS was due to a rumor that an incentive plan was to be introduced (pure nonsense, of course) during which George envisioned huge bonuses. He was convinced that no one could slip an out-of-line figure past him.

Within three months at the IRS George had established a reputation for himself. "The Chase" had been introduced in 1965 by an energetic appointee of a democratic administration. Each morning at six o'clock, a twenty dollar bill was hidden somewhere at the headquarters. Clues consisting of phony expenses such as "coffee and cake at Dino's—$85.00" led to the snack bar. "Parking for meetings—$1,025.00" led to the garage, and so on. This exercise sharpened the wits of the investigators and also led to an extra twenty bucks for the finder.

George excelled and thrilled his fellow employees by seventeen consecutive finds culminating in a recovery of a bill in the bottom of a toilet bowl in the ladies bathroom, precipitated by the clue "bidet for female buyers—$8015.00". He became a legend.

On October 14, 1978 George was handed a choice assignment. The chief called him in for a briefing. "George," he said, "we've got a problem. Henry Albakirk earned 2.5 million dollars last year and paid $400 in income taxes. Something's wrong. It stinks. He bought a new Lexis 400 for 250 dollars and the dealer swears that this represents a viable sale. His wife bought two fur coats valued at $7,000 for 158 bucks and they have the bills to prove it. This guy's been having fun with us and I don't like it. I'm assigning you to this case.—Screw him—make him sweat—and find out what the hell is going on. It's a complete field audit. You'll have as much help as you need."

George was elated…Albakirk was a prize catch, running a business which dealt with city property at fantastic profits, personal income and life style that made New York Magazine, and relatively nothing in the way of income taxes. It stunk, and George was convinced that he alone could purify the smell and clear things up.

Henry Albakirk received the notice of inquiry from the IRS on December 1st, turned it over to his accountants, and promptly flew to San Juan for an extended vacation. After several months of delay the meeting was sat up on February 15th between the lawyers and Fairly.

Fairly entered the offices of Mills and Weber and was immediately impressed by the fine mahogany—paneled walls and green, leather upholstery. A pretty blonde girl greeted him. "Mr. Mills is expecting you, sir. Just down the corridor, first door on the right."

Fairly was not disappointed by the elegant inner offices and expensive accouterments. A highly polished low boy by the window served as a bar containing fine whiskey for important clients. Sam Mills sat at a large, dark—green desk, an assortment of crystal animal figures lined the front edge and served as both distraction and conversation openers. A black leather couch to the right was carefully strewn with a few books and ledgers. This area was cleared when casual conversation was to lead to an important business deal.

Sam rose. "Pleasure to meet you, Mr. Fairly. Would you care for some coffee or tea?"

"No, thank you. I'd prefer to get to work if you don't mind." He was going to get off on the right foot.

Sam frowned for a moment. "Of course," he said, glancing to his left. I believe you are interested in the accounts of Albakirk Enterprises. Anything in particular you'd care to start with?"

"Well, I believe I have your records of payments for the 1987 calendar year. Perhaps we could just take a look at the books of the company for that year so I can familiarize myself with your accounting techniques. Then we'll go from there."

"Of course, of course." Sam pressed a small buzzer and walked toward a paneled door at the rear of the office. He opened it and pointed inside.

"I took the liberty of setting up a desk and calculator for you in here. You may stay as long as you wish. Let me know if you'd care for some lunch or anything else."

A petite young secretary, demurely dressed in simple black, stepped in carrying three large ledgers. She strolled directly into the second office, placed the books on the desk, and pointed to a button. "Anything you wish, sir, just press that."

Very cooperative, thought Fairly. Absolutely first class. He removed his coat and jacket and carefully hung them on the clothes rack alongside the desk. He loosened his tie and began to peruse the ledgers,

Albakirk Enterprises was comprised of three interlocking corporations. Henry Albakirk was chairman of the board of two and president of the third, drawing salaries from all three. There were records of reinvestments, stock options, delayed payments, bank loans, transfers, etc., which occupied most of the morning. While he was interested in the personal income of Albakirk, he thought it might be worthwhile to spend a bit of time on the corporate setup. Maybe there would be material for additional investigation later.

By eleven o'clock he decided to try a few figures. Let's add up some of the income, he thought, and get an idea of the magnitude of the fraud. He was convinced that the set-up was going to be a gold mine of illegal dealings.

He drew one of the leather bound ledgers toward the calculator. He noted it was very heavy, but paid little attention to it. Beautiful covering, he thought. He plugged in the calculator and began to tap lightly on the keys. An electronic display lit up and he quietly jotted a series of numbers down on his lined pad.

By eleven twenty he noticed there was something wrong. He had mentally calculated profits of four million dollars in one three month period, but the display on the calculator lit up 180,000. Must have pressed a minus, he thought. He flipped back several pages and began again. He reached the same point in the calculation and looked at the display which read 58,179. Impossible, he thought. He contemplated starting again and then decided to have some lunch.

He bit into his date-nut sandwich at the lunch counter and thought about the morning's activities. What a dope! Been using calculators for years. How could I make such a mistake,—and a different one each time? Dummy.

By one-thirty he was back at the desk, carefully tapping in the appropriate figures—148328. Two more tries, and two more numbers. He rose and peered out to the larger office. Sam Mills sat at his desk glowering over some reports. A heavy cloud of cigar smoke lay floating on the desk top.

"Excuse me, Mr. Mills, but I think you've got a faulty calculator here."

"Well, wha d'ya know." Sam Mills looked surprised. "Not a very good advertisement for an accountant, and lawyer," he laughed. "We check 'em daily, of course, but I"ll get a new one set up at once."

Within fifteen minutes a shiny new calculator was installed, this one with a memory unit that allowed calculation of complex formulas by a preset program. Fairly set to work at once. A few beads of sweat appeared on his forehead as he entered the numbers. Aha, he smiled, there it is! He had just entered a profit of 729,000 dollars on one sale of a building to the city and looked at the display—a negative 729000. Did he brush across a minus sign instead of adding? He cleared the machine and slowly pressed the digits 7-2-9-0-0-0—It was all right.

Okay, we'll watch that and start over. He slowly entered each figure and satisfied himself that the proper display appeared, then after reaching the final point pressed the 'equal' button: 4,000,000. Hooray, he thought, jotted down the figure and continued a methodical list of entries. He added in the previous profit and pressed the 'equal' button again: 138,079.

"What the hell is going on here?" he said aloud. He heard the desk chair race back, then a short tapping on the door. "Everything's fine, Mr. Mills."

Fairly was deeply disturbed as he left that afternoon and returned to his own office. Those fellows must be buying used calculators, he thought. In order to reassure himself he tapped out a long list of numbers on his own machine, and noted the sum of 7,328,498 which was quite close to the figure he had mentally calculated. "Good," he said.

But that night he was quite distressed. He sat with a large bourbon contemplating the day's activities. A firm the size of Mills and Weber, working with defective machinery? Not very likely. Then what was wrong? Fairly never lacked self-confidence. He prided himself on his sharp mind and astuteness, and above all—his ability to use a calculator. "Too bad they didn't use them in public school," he thought.

Two days later Fairly was back in the little room. For several hours all seemed well as he compiled long lists of figures, but he never came close to the profits he imagined were turned over by these corporations. He decided to try another tack. He peeked through the doorway.

"Excuse me." The dark-haired pretty secretary was arranging several folders on the desk. "Would you be good enough to ask Mr. Mills to prepare the personal expenditures for the 1985 -86 years? I'll go over those next week on my next visit. I would also appreciate it if he would make arrangements for me to bring these ledgers over to the IRS office where I could spend an evening or two with them. I wouldn't want to keep anyone overtime here."

"Of course, Mr. Fairly. I'll make the necessary arrangements personally."

Fairly sat back in his chair once again. He reached into his inside pocket and extracted a small, shiny calculator. He pressed several single digit entries and satisfied that it was working adequately, he opened the first ledger again and began to enter figures.

Profits for the first three months: 169,048.

"Oh my God." the small machine dropped from his hands. He felt the table waver and beads of sweat lined his brow.

He didn't report for work on Friday, taking a long weekend instead. This was the first time he'd missed a day at work. On Monday the chief called him in.

"Fairly, everything okay? You haven't joined 'the chase' this week."

"Fine, chief, fine."

"How's the case going with Albakirk? We're going to get him, nest ce pas, old buddy?"

"Sure but the surface figures look good," he lied. How could he admit what was happening? The sharpest brain in the regional office couldn't get a calculator to add a set of numbers. His hands trembled as he stuffed them into his pockets. He felt faint. He had to get out of there.

That day he couldn't eat. He was trembling when he next appeared at Mills and Weber. He had brought with him a calculator from the office. Over the next week and a half he worked daily at the list of figures before him, working through the IRS calculator and three portable ones that he purchased for the job. Nothing he could do would make the figures add up.

Each time he thought he had the problem licked, a loss would appear where there should have been a profit. He alternated the ledgers, started with number three, then moved to another quarter—but it made no difference.

He finally decided to move out of that room. Mills was as good as his word. He had Albakirk's expenses in a similar ledger and seemed delighted to let Fairly move them over to the IRS offices. Arrangements were made, Fairly signed a receipt, and the ledgers were picked up by two treasury agents for transport to the regional headquarters.

Three weeks passed and his colleagues noticed a change in Fairly. He slouched slightly as he walked, never started a conversation, and had one of the secretaries in tears over a typo which never would have bothered him in the past.

And each night he worked late, almost passionately using a different calculator each time, borrowed from Herman or Jeffreys or one of the other men. He watched them at work during the day and if all seemed to go well, he would borrow their calculator and use it at night.

But nothing helped. Each night he'd press a set of figures, and each night he'd get a different answer.

The final break came on the morning of the fifteenth. Fairly rose especially early that morning and reported for work at 5:30. He slipped into his office and lifted one of the ledgers, placing it under his arm. He walked slowly down several stories to the basement and entered the large computer room. The lights flashed quietly around him as tapes bursting with information rotated on discs.

He sat down at the controls and tapped out a set of instructions. The machines stopped, accepted the program, and then began to whir again softly as he entered figures for a six—month period. He worked with dedication for two hours through the maze of figures, noting the transfers, profits from real estate, a fishing fleet, hotels, race horses.

And the profits ran up, day by day, weekly, monthly grand total for the period : 148,721.

They found him that morning having produced $50,000 in damages to the computer…tapes strewn over the room…lights smashed…They carried him off—the topic of conversation for weeks to come.

On April twenty-first Sam Mills appeared at IRS headquarters and was ushered into the chief's office.

"I know Fairly was one of your best men. I hope he regains his health. I need to know if you intend to pursue the case against my client. After all you must have had interim reports. Two months spent on a few ledgers—can you tell me anything?"

The chief looked down, then across the room. "I guess we'll suspend the inquiry."

"One other thing. If you don't mind," said Sam, I'd like to pick up our records if that's okay."

"Yes, I'll have them waiting for you in the lobby."

Sam carried the four ledgers to the front door and was met by his chauffeur. He sat back calmly in his black Rolls, the ledgers next to him on the seat. He glanced slowly toward them as the car glided through the side streets onto Broadway, heading downtown. He lifted one.

Thank God they never weigh these, he thought. With deliberation he raised one of the ledgers to his ear, opened the cover and listened. He heard the soft hummm of the transistorized motor in the cover. He chuckled. Or x-ray them, he thought. A light flashed on.

"Everything all right, sir?"

"Sure Ed, everything's a-okay." He smiled, replaced the ledger and leaned back.

Chapter X

The Protectors

In any large society there are always those individuals who have a difficult time understanding the way things work. The short cut is anathema to them, and if there is a clearly outlined and longer way to do things, they are sure to find it. Their childhood is marked by inordinate honesty and smug self-satisfaction in being stubbornly adherent to the "right way". Getting on a bus, one young member of this group found a dollar bill lying on a seat. "Anyone lose a dollar?" "Yeah, kid it's mine, Thanks." And the young man is satisfied. Had he kept it himself a rising feeling of guilt would have ensued—because it didn't belong to him.

There is a glowing halo of piousness which surrounds these people. Everybody knows they can be trusted and nobody really likes them. They are tolerated but never become members of the "in" group. They have a great ability to make people around them feel uncomfortable and can always be counted on to cast a dissenting vote. "Going along" is not their cup of tea, and their stubborness is legion. Five boys stand on a corner deciding where to go that night. Four want to split a couple of pizza pies at Don's bar and grill, the fifth doesn't want to. Four end up having pizza, followed by ice cream sodas at Pat's Parlour and the fifth goes home and vomits in his bathroom. He'll be back with the group —always voting for his own way.

Everybody knows that a certain person is best qualified to do a job. He's smart, he has two legs, two arms, two eyes…just like everyone else…But something is missing. They all listen carefully to what he says at club meetings—sure he's right—but he never gets elected to office. He'd rather be right than popular. Having a knack of twinging the conscience of those with whom he congregates, everybody listens to him, agrees with his views, and promptly do as they please. Not the least deterred, he persists in expressing his views, satisfied after stating what is morally correct. But somehow his views are accepted and never acted upon.

In a club meeting he is always the one who knows Robert's Rules of Order—rising to shout out an appropriate "point of order" or noting that a vital amendment wasn't approved by the seconder. He is a thorn in the side of progress.

In a free society there are those individuals who aren't making it. Always investing in a stock market at a peak, or buying a used car that had been totaled three weeks previously. These poor souls have a need to complain. Writing their congressman usually brings a standard, formal response. They need a champion. The "good government" advocate, the consumer protector,—our young man, described above, who will rant and rave at the system and take up the cudgel for those who can't get along within it.

He plays an important role, and in dealing with him those in power are sure to let him have his way just enough times to serve as a safety valve, blowing off enough steam from time to time to keep the pot from boiling over. Working in a small office, usually in Washington, wearing suits bought off plain pipe racks,—usually on sale—he has the ear of Congress, the press, administrators, and businessmen, who listen, admire, agree, but never seem to act on his ideas.

If he ever ran for Congress his most ardent advocates wouldn't vote for him. After all the people may complain about government insensitivity, but when alone in the voting booth they are sure to choose the men who can work with the system and get things done. It's one thing to complain about contamination of tuna fish, but quite another to let someone close the canning factory and do away with your job.

Within the system the businessman, who is after all the epitome of the free institutions and the focus of real admiration, learns not only to tolerate our protector but in many instances to use him to good advantage. But that's the way it's supposed to work—isn't it?

The Consumer's Good Angel

Vinnie Serrano grew up in a shaded residential area of the city, free from the hum of busy streets, subways and crowded stores. He was the second of four children, loved for his curly black hair, languid brown eyes, and quiet disposition. He seemed never to complain, but studied, ate and slept without a whine or whimper according to the household rules.

His father was a studious man with a degree in biochemistry and a rank of assistant professor at a local community college. His greatest ambition was to gather the knowledge, publications and accompanying plaudits that would allow him to rise to the rank of full professor. Then he needn't contend with appearing before classes of dummies any more, but could spend his time writing obscure memos and attending national meetings. Tenure was a wonderful goal.

At the age of twelve a major crisis arose in Vinnie's life. His friend, Alfred, was the first to notice. It was a Friday after lunch when Vinnie appeared to be limping while leaving the cafeteria.

"What's up, Vinnie? You break a leg or something?"

"No, forget it."

The weekend passed quietly but on Monday afternoon Alfred noticed that Vinnie was stooping somewhat when he walked. It was eight days later when Vinnie confided in his buddy.

"It's that Puglia bastard. He thinks I've been eyeing his sister or something. Anyway, he doesn't like me. Every day for a week he's been waiting for me on the way to school on Sample Avenue. When I pass, he hauls off and smacks me in the stomach."

"For cryin' out loud. He's too big to fight you. Why don't you tell your father?"

"I ain't givin' in. I didn't do anything wrong and I've got as much right to be on Sample Avenue as he has."

"Look, Vinnie, cut across old man Dougherty's lot. Nobody uses it and you'll end up near the school. Puglia'll never know, it's way out of the way for him."

"No way. I didn't do nothin' wrong. Besides that'd be trespassing."

"What're you talking about? Old man Dougherty doesn't care who walks on his lot. He likes kids."

"No way—he can't keep me from using the street. I'm entitled as much as him."

"He'll kill ya."

*   *   *

Mrs. Serrano was upset. "Tony you've got to talk to Vinnie."

"What?"

"It's Vinnie. Something's wrong. He doesn't eat anymore."

Vinnie's mother was an Americanized Italian, first generation, which meant ideas, desires and emotions she found hard to reconcile with what she found herself doing most of the time. She was caught between the old world and the new, spending her hours in the kitchen, having babies, just like her mother and grandmother. She wasn't part of the credit card corps of women who had special parking spaces at all the malls in the area. Having lunch in town with her friends was an activity she denied herself, in spite of her wishes, blaming the small income commensurate with her husband's salary; but secretly yearning to break away, admiring the new outfits and mod appearances of her neighbors. She found solace in raising he four children, settling for family allegiance, and the comfortable feeling of belonging, constantly suppressing thoughts which rose to the surface each time she dressed and looked at her still youthful body.

She stood at the butcher block cutting board, dicing and preparing the evening meal. Two large pots boiled busily on the stove and the oven was turned on—awaiting the introduction of the sliced veal.

Her husband looked at her through the kitchen doorway, not stepping over the threshold he responded: "What? What's going on?"

"I'm telling you, Tony, he's either sick or something's wrong. Please talk to him. Maybe he's worried about something."

"Sure, okay. Vinnie! Come here for a minute"

Within the hour, Theresa Sorrano heard her husband's footsteps crossing into the kitchen. He stepped quietly toward the kitchen table, pulled a squeaky chair out, and sat down, his chin resting in his palm. "Theresa, you won't believe this—you won't believe it for a minute."

"What's wrong, what is it?"

"I can't believe it myself."

"What, Tony, what?"

"Some big kid's been waiting for Vinnie on the way to school every day. When he passes by, the kid winds up and smacks Vinnie in the stomach."

"Oh Tony, why didn't he tell you before?" she turned the gas flame down and walked over to her husband.

"He won't let me interfere. He says he knows his rights, and he's entitled to the same streets the other kid is."

"Tony—you've got to do something—he could be hurt."

"I know, but he won't let me see the kid. I'll tell you something else you won't believe." Tony turned his chair toward his wife and faced her directly.

"What?"

"I told him to go to school another way, like crossing the Dougherty property. He'd bypass the kid and end up near the school."

"So—what did he say?"

"He won't walk on Dougherty's grass!"

Theresa grasped the edge of the table, and sat down. She looked as though a major catastrophe had struck. It was a response she reserved for all negative news, regardless of the severity. Tony on the other hand seemed to find a bit of humor in the whole situation.

"Oh my God," she said, "I don't believe it."

"Listen Theresa, I spent an hour talking to Vinnie and I've come to one conclusion."

"What's that?"

"Either that big kid gets tired of hitting him in the stomach,—or Vinnie's going to starve to death!"

*   *   *

Years later Vinnie remembered the Puglia episode as he stepped into the elevator of the large public building. He pressed the button for the seventh floor. He had won out by stubborn persistence. Puglia tired of the whole affair as suddenly as it had started. Determination had won after all. Doing the right thing became a fetish and won the admiration of his friends and later his colleagues. That's what people needed—a model—someone to show them the right way—to stand up to the short cuts. His rule was clear, he would protect them from their own inadequacies.

His office was simply furnished. His secretary, Mrs. Amy Pratt sat in a small anteroom at a light brown wooden desk that gave the appearance of teak, but was actually a less expensive veneer. A computer sat at the corner of the desk with the screen angled so she could see it easily. A keyboard sat directly in front of her and a telephone, a large rolodex and a dictating machine on a large clear plastic pad were stratigically placed for easy access. The printer and fax machine sat on their separate stands, and two large vertical metal files stood like guards along the wall. There was only room for one chair in addition to the one occupied by Mrs. Pratt.

Vinnie's office was only slightly larger. In addition to the usual computer, phone and printer he hung his college degree laminated in walnut on the wall along with several posters announcing the openings of Giselle and Swan Lake which he adored.

His desk was clearly purchased at the same clearance sale as Mrs. Pratt's.

Vinnie had arrived in Washington several years earlier as an assistant to a major consumer advocate who subseqently died at 3 A.M. one Thursday in the arms of his secretary. His wife insisted that he often worked late. The only problem was explaining why there was no computer in the motel where he was found.

Vinnie with six years experience took over. Of course with a new secretary carefully selected by his mother, the now venerable Theresa. His files were teeming with frauds, secret price fixings, rotten meat, infected eggs, and any other risk to society. Now he was working on the auto industry.

With the help of a series of carefully orchestrated press conferences he could apply significant pressure, or at least a modicum of embarassment on the congress. The press loved a juicy story and Vinnie supplied them regularly.

The major entrepreneurs in the nation had to consider Vinnie's reaction to a new product as part of the cost of doing business. Naturally they looked forward to beating him.

One day, Mrs. Pratt rushed into his office. A messenger had delivered a note for Vinnie. It was from John Devlin executive vice president of the largest auto producer in the U.S. It read:

Dear Mr.Serrano,

I am personally requesting that you visit our offices. We wish to discuss any problems that may arise in our new models. I believe that your recent criticism may be worth discussing. I hope that this will not be an inconvenience.

Sincerely

Miles Devlin

Vinnie was impressed. The meeting was set up by Mrs. Pratt and Devlin's secretary.

Devlin's company owned their own building in New York. It was a massive structure of 96 floors containing not only offices, but also a large private restaurant, a hall for affairs such as large dinners for the President, weddings, or other special occasions, a gym, pool, and indoor private driving range.

Devlin had arranged for Vinnie to be picked up and flown to New York on the company's private plane. Vinnie however took a taxi to National Airport and the shuttle.

As he exited the elevators on the 74th floor he entered through large glass doors, approaching a huge desk. A lovely young girl pressed the button on the intercom.

"Mr. Vincent G. Serrano, sir." she announced.

"Yes, of course."

A slightly built, dapper man greeted him. Devlin himself. Vinnie observed the fine cut of his dark blue pinstripe suit as he was led through a doorway into a larger room.

"Mr. Sorrano, a pleasure to see you. Please take a seat here. May I get you a drink or a smoke?"

"No, I don't do either." Vinnie had pictured the office in his mind many times. He almost thought he could recognize each particle of furniture, the lithographs on the walls, the small statues. Only the exact identifying features needed to be filled in. The furniture was teak, real teak—the lithographs were impressionist.

"Please make yourself comfortable. I realize this meeting is a bit awkward—but I thought it be valuable if we had a meeting of the minds. Perhaps I could indicate some of the factors affecting our point of view."

"Three people were killed last week, Mr. Devlin."

"I understand, Mr. Sorrano. We don't know whether the accidents precipitated the deaths directly or whether the hood locks…"

"Mr. Devlin, we need to be more direct. We both know that the hood on your car is defective. The problem exists in each of your models on the road today. You can't seriously deny it."

"I realize your point of view tends to be somewhat dramatic—of necessity, of course. You must be in a position to influence the press. And of course, big business is the bad guy. I accept that, Mr. Sorrano, we're each entitled to our own corner. I hoped you would consider some other points that are involved.

"We represent over six million employees," he continued, "You know our problems with the congress. We are committed to clean air—anti pollution devices that must be in every model within two years. The cost is astounding. The automobile industry at full employment will be operating at a dead loss for the next two years just to pay for the changeovers. If we announce a recall of six hundred thousand automobiles now to repair the hood lock, it would mean a loss of confidence that could cost us several hundred thousand sales next year. Coupled with our design commitments, a loss of two million jobs is inevitable. Please understand!"

"Mr. Devlin, you must forgive me for being dense. When your cars are impacted at ten miles per hour, the hood flies up and crashes through the front windshield. We have tested models over and over and the findings are inescapable. There's a defect in the hood lock. Many people—"

"I know, I know, and I understand your position as a consumer advocate. But in life we frequently have to balance many things—often to reach a compromise."

"Mr. Devlin, if you know me, you know that compromise—"

"Mr. Sorrano," Devlin was quick to break in, "please consider an alternative. We have been after Congress to postpone the requirements for the anti-pollution devices for an additional two years. This would enable us to complete a recall, repair all the hoods, and buffer our profits until the inevitable clean—air standards are met. We would also avoid having the unemployment attributed to your...any organization."

"I'm not in favor of dirty air, Mr. Devlin."

"I understand. But think of it this way. Instead of unemployment versus a possible highway death, it's unemployment versus two more years of mild contamination. Certainly that's not as likely to make a significant health impact—as might large—scale unemployment."

Vinnie quieted down. He thought a moment. Add up the pluses and minuses. He would get credit for the recall. Many lives would be saved. He couldn't be a hero when jobs were at stake, especially if his organization might get blamed.

He glanced out of the window onto a magnificent view of the city. The East River wound around the curve of lower Manhattan. Tiny cars, in a solid line, crept along the Drive.

"You drive a hard compromise. I won't take an active part in any of this, you know."

"Right, Mr. Serrano, right! Just take the pressure off your congressional colleagues—that's all. We'll take care of the rest. Don't make any comments either way. We'll fix the hoods, you get the credit, and we save jobs."

"Good day, Mr. Devlin. It was a pleasure meeting you."

A secretary appeared to guide Vinnie out of the elaborate office and then returned.

"This Mr. Serrano," she asked, "is he as obstinate as his reputation says?"

"Even more, my dear…even more. He requires special handling. Otherwise we'd make him a vice-president of the company."

*   *   *

It was seven p.m. when the guests began arriving. The long, oak conference table could not be recognized for it was covered with a white, lace table cloth. Bowls of ice and mounds of beaded caviar with the usual accompaniments of butter, eggs and onions were placed carefully about. Champagne bottles, imported iced vodka and scotch lined the side boards. Two dozen finely dressed men milled about, shaking hands.

"A toast to Miles!"

A loud hum and then muted applause.

"Thank you, gentlemen, thank you."

"Devlin, you did a fantastic job. How did you work it out?"

"Trade secrets, Stevens—we can't give them all away."

"But he's such an ass."

"Tch, tch, Stevens, don't criticize our benefactor in such a callous way."

"How much do we save?"

"Over a billion the first year. With the two—year delay that's quite a bundle."

"Devlin, old fellow,—mind telling us what the next battle is on this? Congress wants to hold off, but they need a reason. How do we go from here?"

"Have no fear, sir, have no fear. By the time the clean air bill comes up again we'll be up to our next model changeover. We've already completed the plans for the new design. It's excellent. You must see the construction of the left front door—guaranteed to swing open on impact."

"Wonderful, wonderful."

"Yes. We'll be prepared for our next appointment with the avenger.

Epilogue

A Vote For The People

As with all treatises that clarify fundamental aspects of life, I do not expect that the majority of my readers will benefit significantly from this book. After all, we are slaves of our environment and genes and it is unlikely that any major changes in human nature can be wrought in a short period of time. Don't be upset by this pessimistic outlook. The same would be true for books on the profits in the stock market or real estate killings. Remember that for an individual or institution to make a big stock profit by selling at the top of the market, there must be a number of poor average souls buying at the top of the market. Alas, it is the fate of the majority to serve the unique purpose of helping the few to make it big.

But for the system to succeed it is necessary for the public to perceive the possibility of ready access. Hopefully the average man can make it (obviously there's not a chance in the world that the average man can make it), and this perception is strengthened from time to time by examples of individuals from poor backgrounds, who do in fact, make it big. Needless to say these are distinctive and unusual persons who possess unlimited imagination, drive and guts. Let's not criticize the average person, however, because he sees himself as his own hero. Hope keeps everything on an even keel.

Getting back to our general thesis of the value of corruption in the free society, we have not fully examined two aspects of the problem: that is the mechanisms necessary to keep the society free, and the provision of appropriate outlets engendering the myth of participation. Both will be discussed in the following paragraphs.

Exercising One's Freedom

Voting:

Let's dispose of this right off! In a free society opportunities to vote must be provided periodically, but everyone knows it really doesn't make any difference who is elected. The more offices that are elective, the more freedom appears to exist, but the characters running for these posts usually are buddies of certain entrenched corruptor such as those we've met earlier in this book. How else could the candidates get the money it costs to run for office. As a matter of fact, local elections in certain urban areas are rumored to consist of the same individual running under two different names. Speaking of names, the first requirement of running for local office is to have the right name for the particular locality. This is the leading characteristic used by voters to evaluate the qualifications of the candidates.

As we move up the scale of state and national elections, the difference between candidates changes very little. It is important to maintain a two—party system to enhance the myth that there really is a choice. However, in order to attract a majority of voters, true differences of opinion must be blunted. Most knowledgeable corruptors will support each party, anyhow.

The informed electorate recognizes right off that voting is a futile exercise in a free society and therefore most refuse to participate. As a matter of fact, there is an inverse relationship between the general intelligence of the electorate of a country and the percent of eligible voters voting.

The Cocktail Forum

This is where true democracy in action can be found. Politics discussed at a local barroom reaches the epitome of sophistication and enables the participants unlimited expression, unlimited, that is, assuming all weapons are checked at the door. Recognized as the place most voters would rather be, some governments have tried to close these establishments on election day, only to be frustrated by having the forum move to a nearby apartment. There's nothing like two or three vodka martinis to clarify the issues in any election, or to create the impression that some exist.

Buying One's Congressman

The going rate in the present market is about $25,000 to $50,000 per year depending on the number of committees he or she belongs to. This establishes the value of committee appointments in Congress. This amount is out of the reach of the average citizen, who's probably not interested anyway, unless there is a significant amount to be gained by a certain vote. One vote won't help anyhow. State senators and local judges can be obtained at much cheaper rates.

This is only recommended as an investment for those with guaranteed profits. Large corporations have worked out the price lists in detail and get it as a tax break to boot.

It was suggested once, as a method of assuring true representation, that an attempt be made to buy all of the Congress. To this end a fund was established consisting of a donation of one dollar per person yielding a total way in excess of 250,000,000 dollars. This was considered adequate to purchase the entire Congress and four cabinet directors to boot. The purchase having been proposed, no two people in the organization could agree on what issues they wanted Congress to vote. For a few thousand extra, the individual senators were back in the open market, thus destroying what was a spectacular plan of providing a voice for the people in the government.

The only way to get into the system is to develop a one—issue group, supported by membership contributions sufficient to make the appropriate purchases and guaranteeing a certain vote. This, of course, has been frequently done in the past and continues to be an important method of exercising one's freedom.

I hope this book was worthwhile reading and provided insight into the mechanisms that affect our daily lives. Perhaps we cannot each take advantage of the many devices described, but at least we can hope that we've obtained an understanding.

www.ingramcontent.com/pod-product-compliance
Lightning Source LLC
Chambersburg PA
CBHW031242280526
45784CB00004B/1687